Editorial Director USA
Pierantonio Giacoppo

Chief Editor of Collection
Maurizio Vitta

Publishing Coordinator
Franca Rottola

Translations
Martyn Anderson

Graphic design
CREA Studio, Milano

Photographs
Eduard Hueber, Paul Warchol

Colour separation
Litofilms, Bergamo

Printing
Poligrafiche Bolis, Bergamo

First published April 1997

ISBN 88-7838-039-3

Resolution: 4 Architecture

Resolution:4 Architecture

An Idea of a Site Text

*Introduction by
Mario Antonio Arnaboldi*

l'ARCAEDIZIONI

Contents

Architects' Statement: Stray Paths

Some Notes on the Idea of a Site Text

After having worked several years in "name" offices, we have formed a partnership in 1990 that is concerned with establishing a critical practice based on both practical and theoretical issues. While at these well-established offices, we have participated in the tried and true practice of stressing product over process, the known over the unfamiliar, the form over the formation. It is with this professional background that we turn our focus to the design process. This concentration might best be described as investigations down "stray paths", without on emphasis on a preconceived end-product.

What does it mean to practice architecture critically in an age of informations? The ability to access information at any time is reframing our traditional context. No longer can our belief systems exist within a single frame of reference or be seen from a privileged point of view. The myth of the singular heroic architect is dead. Familiar products have been perpetuated by the comfortable process of design and its connoisseurship. The need for multiple readings and meanings exists. Our response to this new age is embodied in our exploration of the production of an architecture.

Our stray path focus has been on the re-analysis, re-interpretation and re-presentation of existing "essential information".

Our experiments are woven within the intentions of the design process, a blurring of the privileged frame of reference. Our re-interpretation of this blurring is what we call a "Site Text", created through a process of superposition, of layering, of analogous elements and ideas through specific registrations.

The production of an architecture can be described as the continuous process of layering, copying and tracing of information. For us, this process of creation is read as a text that becomes a (destabilized) foundation for the projects' conceptual landscape. This fabricated text is sometimes viewed as a series of scaled relationships that are slipped, dislocated, cut, folded and reregistered, suggesting a process of formation not possible without this type of operative.

The production of a Site Text is a process that allows us to participate with each project's specific context, while not being imprisoned by the "contextual" in the privileged traditional sense. We believe in the study and understanding of an architectural history in that we can refer to and defer from it: NOT to be policed or governed by it. This method of our "stray path" excursions has shown us that the formal representation of architecture, when dislocated from the constraints of nostalgia and history, becomes a process that is fluid, non-linear, and unpredictable.

The following projects attempt to reveal latent form-generating issues by re-analyzing each project's inherent "context". Our reading of this edited information is screened through a series of initial analyses, which is then re-

recorded and re-analyzed becoming the raw material for the transmission of a Site Text. In other words, it is a new network, or matrix, of information uncovered through the "art of making copies" from other forms of information. The resolution of the text allows us to explore issues of form-making that could be viewed as outside of the traditional realm of production, while within the realm of architecture. This blurs the starting or reference point and can trigger new combinations and permutations, especially when contaminated with an architectural program. The fold or juncture between text and program also becomes a stray path investigation in as much as this becomes a dialogue between the project's general and specific attributes. It is here that the residue of specificity in each individual project emerges. The re-interpretation of this information into a two-dimensional graphic allows us a format to explore traditional readings of each "site", while at the same time it invites readings from other points of view. Other readings of the Site Text extend beyond the (implied) boundaries of its (imprinted) cover, referring and deferring to its past and future conditions, while suspended in a constant state of becoming. The process of the Site Text's "present", although never yet *final* state, is re-presented as the architectural project. The simultaneity of readings within each project is an attempt to prevent one singular or privileged reading, thus re-framing each project's "con-text" within this Information Age.

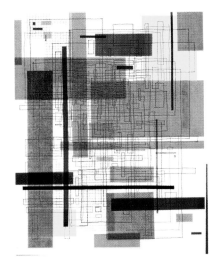

Resolution:4 Architecture

Introduction by Mario Antonio Arnaboldi

Architectural design exerts a considerable influence on the destiny of mankind: it provides a service and, at the same time, is projected towards its own renewal within the profession of architecture itself.

The recently established design practice known as Resolution: 4, which could either be interpreted as "fourth resolution" or, considering the kind of work it carries out, "designers of the fourth dimension", is seeking to create a new form of architecture for newly emerging populations of varying sizes and cultures with different standards of living and balances of life.

One of the practice's most interesting design narratives is the World Park project in Perth, Australia, a disturbingly uneasy tale of expansion reflected in both their minds as architects and sensitivity as human beings. These young architects use architectural experimentation to investigate the possibilities of a new dimension of living/economics. This is less evident in their smaller projects, since they evidently need wide open spaces to express their ideas. Still, this does not prevent them from analyzing gradually evolving human behavioural patterns and their implications on technology. Any truly representative picture of Resolution: 4 and their team work must inevitably focus on those factors weighing most heavily on their design and planning techniques.

One of the most vivid examples of this design method is the architectural idea underpinning the Wainaku Mill Hotel project in Hilo, Hawaii.

This project is both a form of experimentation and, at the same time, at the service of experimentation, in perfect harmony with the most recent analyses of economists, sociologists, and political commentators. In other words, the key to their work lies in the way they cater for the combined effects of both technological and economic progress; and the peculiar way they manage to draw out intriguing design conclusions, particularly in their large-scale projects.

It ought, in fact, to be pointed out that the average individual income in major consumer societies is actually increasing, although the gap between the rich and poor has remained the same; on the other hand, products and consumption, which are capable of promoting people up the social ladder, inevitably lead to a state of notable anxiety due to growing expectations.

Growing expectations and the increase in the amount of leisure time available have, in this respect, inevitably caused young people to grow up more quickly in what is becoming an increasingly permissive society.

This rather incomplete picture of the developing trends in contemporary society leads us into a more careful analysis of Resolution: 4's evolving experimentation. It is worth examining just what makes the team tick on a creative level. They have got a clear idea of what it takes to create new cities capable of encompassing changes in the working environment/population and of harnessing the transformations required to gear urban planning to innovation. A form of innovation grounded in a union of various different scientific practices and designed to celebrate social life as an expression of modernity. These New York-based architects also pay careful attention to not making indiscriminate use of technological progress. They draw on experimentation to create a modern way of living and intervene in production to lay the grounds for the most appropriate style of contemporary community life.

They seem to be striving to give contemporary life its own characteristic identity by designing territorial structures epitomizing the society in which we live; structures projected towards the future instead of just copying the lifeless remains of old-fashioned styles.

Their projects are reminiscent of the way in which Guy Debord describes the spectacular evolution of Western society in *The Entertainment Society*, claiming that art has now gained the upper hand over philosophy. This is in fact true. I have pointed out on several occasions that contemporary thought has inverted its priorities from "art-philosophy" to "philosophy-art", since, in the past, classicism, the Renaissance, the seventeenth century, and other later developments, found a common denominator in the symmetry of parts. This vision has now changed. Nowadays, attention is no longer focused on modernism, postmodernism, relativism, Ptolemaic decadence or Calvinism.

Violence and indifference have now given way to negotiation, we have become the champions of transparency against public squander and the fear of major enterprises. Generally speaking, society is against any form of dictatorship or demagogic regime, setting its sights on a new notion of virtue. The centre, which used to be a starting point, is now a destination that can only be reached through careful meditation and a common grounding of sentiment and feeling. The collapse of old-fashioned academic institutions and classical systems is bringing with it a decadent form of symmetry. Resolution: 4 is well aware of all this, which is why it is opposed to the recycling of the dictates of the past. They have totally abandoned symmetry, which is merely emphasized as being a result of the new notion of space which, as they well know, Euclid, Einstein and Mandelbrot helped to create, as if simulation were to take the place of reality.

In the wake of this rush of thought, Resolution: 4 has once again demonstrated its awareness of the fact that "contemporary ideas" are like a cluster of crystals which, as part of a system, have a superior level of symmetry that almost seems to correspond to some greater system. This system of thought provides the framework within which their design work tends towards a common core of intents; it is as if they had freed themselves from a scholastic conception of planning and design. Both Westerners and Orientals at the same time, they are fundamentally part of the hemisphere but not in any absolute sense.

Nature and culture are fused together in their idea of architectural design, as their weariness of old-fashioned culture stretches to the extreme; it is as if their projects can really sense the transition from libraries to video-libraries, as the space of learning dissolves into time. It is time that marks the surpassing of preservation as it takes on the symbolic value of annulment. The underlying ideology of their new projects and the basic mode of presentation and implementation of their state-of-the-art production is deeply entrenched in this background scenario of events. This new "elliptical form" of classicism they are appropriating derives directly from their peculiar sense of artistry.

The mathematical thought underpinning these young architects' work produces forms of great simplicity; when the Resolution: 4 team envisages a city or an entire territory for the future, paying due attention to the latest technological developments, their thoughts take on a distinctly elliptical configuration. These are the foundations on which it grounded its project for the Nara Convention Hall in Japan. The project hinges around an ellipsoidal layout in which the sum (not difference) of the distances of each architectural function from two fixed points is a constant. This determines a new form that allows both time and energy to be saved in day-to-day living. The design seems to curve space and each point along its unextended line is located at a point inside a circle and ellipse, which represent the curved spaces describing the underlying layout of the entire complex. In other words, numbers ultimately play a decidedly functional role in determining its shape and structure.

The "forms" of their projects are not just fanciful whims of incompetent architects, they are actually the inevitable consequence of the intellectual, social and technical conditions of the age in which we and they live. Like genuinely "competent" architects they draw their new forms from everyday life and present them as fundamental departures from the past. They know that they have to break with the past if they are to project design into the age in which we live, using new technology to lay the foundations of a new society. They also know that they must abandon old-fashioned styles once and for all, if we are to rediscover our purity of spirit and elaborate new forms of awareness. Resolution: 4 draws on these phenomena to shake the general public out of its indifference in an attempt to convince us that the problems associated with architecture have real consequences for our lives, determining changes in our public and private behavioural patterns. Combating mannerism in the name of individual style must be a categorical imperative for society as a whole, if we are to prevent cities from becoming architectural replicas that pay no attention whatsoever to context or tradition. This New York-based team seems to be well aware of these problems, which is why, despite the difficulty of the task at hand, it has decided to try and invent its own new architectural style.

The projects it has so far designed show no sign of the crisis in which rationalism is supposed to be floundering. On the contrary, they are concrete evidence that, despite its "age", rationalism still has a guiding role to play in the name of tradition. Modernity, that promised so much, is also an "unfinished project", if, as Nietzsche insisted, it "draws us away from our origins" and takes the joy out of life. As Heidegger pointed out, far from putting people in command, the essence of technology is something which man, by his very nature, just cannot control.

Resolution: 4's projects show that the idea of modernity may also be a nightmare, as epitomized by contemporary society itself. Habermas described it as "a deceitful symbiosis" between rational forms of life and technological control of nature which, according to him, "has swept the criticism of modernity onto the agenda". Recapturing time, according to Ilia Prigogine, is a revolutionary act of Copernican proportions: instead of treating the irreversible phenomena surrounding us as due to our approximations in describing nature, we need to incorporate them in mechanics and alter the way we represent the laws of dynamics, which ought to be a study into the evolving probabilities of any given system. As we examine Resolution: 4's projects, we can see how they are trying to weaken the grip of functionalism on design in order to link together factors related to knowledge and aesthetics, thereby diminishing the impact of reason without discarding it altogether. Their designs derive from instability, nostalgically evoking the critical attack on the International Style, dating back to Foster, that ought to have carried the project of modernity to its conclusion. It is Habermas's "hope that has changed beyond all recognition" that may allow us to glimpse signs of a breakdown in the crisis of existence.

This is, of course, a utopian dream, but it not less certainly an that intriguing thing about the projects designed by this team of young New York architects is their deep understanding of the great world of Architecture. It is their ideas about "chaos", Benoît Mandelbrot's new interpretation of mathematics, and René Thom's theory of catastrophe, that radically transform traditional approaches to design into a different vision of architecture. It would be rather naive to think that they can shake off all previous assumptions and construct their own "in vitro" theory of knowledge; in actual fact they merely confine themselves to effecting semiological readings.

Our new age of classicism depends on new means of controlling and determining thought: we have moved beyond modernity into a different vision of the interaction between nature and culture. But is this enough to surpass modernity or, in other words, exercise "the evil spirit of unstoppable progress", the ghost that Horkheimer and Adorno contrasted with the Enlightenment and that Michel Foucault re-evoked in his "unmasking" of human sciences? This is perhaps what we really need to known if we are to construct that new linguistic-practical conceptual scheme within which Resolution: 4 is trying to find some way of grounding a new classical spirit.

We need to insist on the role that these designers have confiscated for their own purposes, a role of dissent and of creating a new idiom projecting them on to those fundamental values capable of grounding in sentiment the newly emerging strands of knowledge destined to shape our future.

These philosophical investigations only go to show what a daunting task they have set themselves, how deeply involved in architecture they actually are, and what a great responsibility history has placed on their shoulders. We might advise them that the most "human" thing they can do is to carry on voicing their deeply held beliefs as simply and sensibly as possible and to accept their consequences. This architectural responsibility will, of course, make them vulnerable to others. It should also be pointed out that the richness of architectural history has allowed them to express their own design language with great spontaneity. The way they have trampled on conventions is reminiscent of a great name from the past: Leon Battista Alberti, a notable scholar of architecture who managed to find the right balance between aesthetics and ethics, technology and invention, the power of creativity and the rational techniques underpinning architecture. Burckhardt drew on this legacy in his *Italian Renaissance Art* that elaborates on Alberti's concept of "concinnitas" (measure and elegance). The list of words that various authors have employed in trying to express the true contents of architecture is almost endless. Technique and linguistics or alternatively utility and beauty are just more key words that seem to allow us to treat the principles of design as an imaginary "invention". Resolution: 4 and its designers' mathematical reading of architecture allows them to set up a constant state of interaction between theory and arithmetical practice that produces a continually evolving socio-economic system around which to organize project themes.

There are words that naturally lead on to a certain line of thinking and words that guide the decision-making process. But attention also needs to be focused on the way in which they give voice to the kind of technology that is currently transforming the image of architectural design. These words can ideally be transferred into the newly emerging worlds of virtual reality, a disturbing chapter in the history of computer science that can stimulate the kind of mental and corporeal experiences associated with drugs. Resolution: 4's projects seem to belong to this new paradigm. Their buildings seem to embody the paradox Timothy Leary first announced in his *Cyberspace*: expressing a creative potential of great aesthetic-political import. They represent a sort of co-existence between mysticism and industrial society forged into a state of high technology. The architects of Resolution: 4 have already moved beyond McLuhan's electrical revolution. All this means that they operate in the world of experimentation, and the images they design provide a real contribution to the artistic background against which they are created. We know that physical reality is governed by precise laws. But we also know that this kind of experimentation into artificial reality can shake the laws of physics at their very foundations. We are now in a position to actually eliminate the gravity acting on bodies and create imaginary worlds that are perfectly credible. The question is just why does virtual reality naturally come to mind when analyzing Resolution: 4's projects? The answer is that their work latently, but no less genuinely, embodies a process already projected into the near future.

Their projects naturally call for this kind of critical analysis, drawing, as they do, on the latest tools and instruments available to anybody interested in the concept of architectural space. I am mainly referring to the use of computer technology, that takes perception well beyond the limits we are accustomed to, and newly emerging high-tech tools such as lasers or telematics that turn out to be fabulous interpretative "media". Reality, on the other hand, is increasingly governed by micro-electronics that enable material to be used with infinitely greater precision than before and in ways which are beyond our usual realms of perception. The use of materials and the scale of form and function have now entered a quite different economic dimension. This is why the architects of Resolution: 4 have abandoned the idea of ornamental decoration, inevitably associated with refined elegance and technological intuition. Their architectural space is geared to an electronically-determined minimalist reading of space. Examining their projects with careful attention, we can see how they tend to move beyond the idea of generating forms governed by some sort of figurative weight of gravity, thereby taking space beyond space itself; some sort of coded reading of a situation or environment mediating between feeling and artifice. The spatio-temporal patterns governed by relativity under the control of micro-electronics produce quite surprising results. It is easy to imagine how their representations of space are moving further and further away from old archetypes of rational-functional forms. Their artistry exploits the language of mathematics to project their creative intuition into the future, leaving the recent past at its heels. It is only fitting to conclude this critical reading of the work of Resolution: 4 with a quote from Leon Battista Alberti: *"Architettore chiamo io colui il quale saprà, con certa e meravigliosa ragione e regola, sà con la mente e con l'animo divisare, sà con l'opera recare a fine tutte quelle cose le quali, mediante movimenti di pesi, congiungimenti ed ammassamenti di corpi, si possono con gran dignità accomodare benissimo allo uso delli uomini"*.

Works

Wainaku Mill Hotel

Location: Hilo, Hawaii
Date of Design: 1990
Program: 300 Room Health
Resort, 300 Room
Conference Center,
Japanese Cultural Center,
Restaurants, Gardens
Principals: Joseph Tanney,
Robert Luntz, Gary
Shoemaker, Paul Boardman
Project Team: Kai Chui,
David Fratianne, Kong
Yuang, Bryce Sanders,
Amar Sen
Modelmaker: Paul Steiner
Structural Engineers:
Severud Associates:
Ed Massina, Ed Depaola
Consulting Engineers:
Jaros Baum & Bolles:
Mitch Simpler

This project is the Wainaku Mill Hotel in Hilo, Hawaii. The highly visible 12 acre site is at the Ale'alea Point, on Hilo Bay, and is the location of an abandoned sugar processing facility. The program consists of a combined 300 room health/recreation resort hotel, a 300 room business/conference center hotel and a 50,000 sq. ft. cultural center for the visual and performing arts, as well as tropical gardens, traditional Japanese baths and health amenities, retail galleries and restaurants.

The Big Island of Hawaii is divided along its north-south axis by a volcanic ridge. The site's existing ridge, created by the lava flows, establishes a line which divides the parcel with a north-south axis. This division is reinforced by the location of the island's perimeter loop road. The coastline was displaced by the pressure of the lava wash breaking through the line, creating a gap between the ridge and the coast. This gap is marked by an existing seawall and defines Ale'alea Point and a black sand beach.

The architectonic investigation explores the nature of the interval between these scaled site conditions. The elements which act as formal catalysts to the architectural diagram are the lava ridge, the existing overpass, the existing service tunnel, and the sea. The manipulation and abstraction of these elements creates a series of layers on the site. To mark the north south division and reinforce the nature of the coastline, these layers are first consolidated into the singular gesture of a "wall". The overpass is extended, penetrating and shearing the barrier just created, linking the site and revealing the major program divisions.

Intervals in scale are linked to the found elements in dimension and position. The existing service tunnel marks the line upon which the north-south shear occurs, locates the main hotel site circulation and sets the dimension of the typical hotel block, articulating the "wall". The focus of the hotels are created by sheared and dis-placed layers of the "wall". One such layer, registered along the sea wall, contains the conference facility. Another layer located along the loop road, forms the project portal. The bridge spans the layers of the site and becomes the link to the cultural center. This center, as the literal piece dislocated by the lava wash, becomes a Hookopu, the traditional ti leaf wrapped rock offering to the volcano goddess.

Aerial perspective.

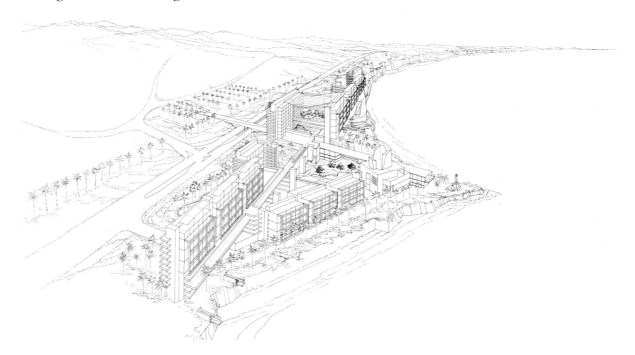

Far left, view from north; left, view from loop road showing existing overpass.

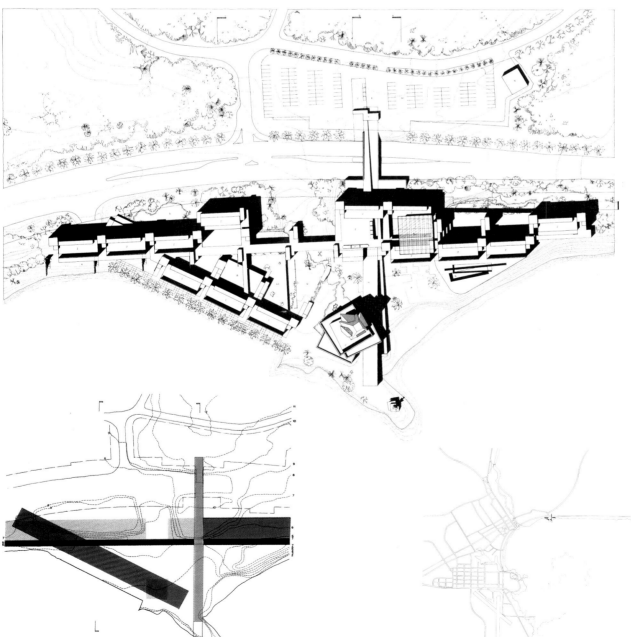

Shadowed site plan and, below, site diagram and location plan.

Floor plan of entry gate
level.

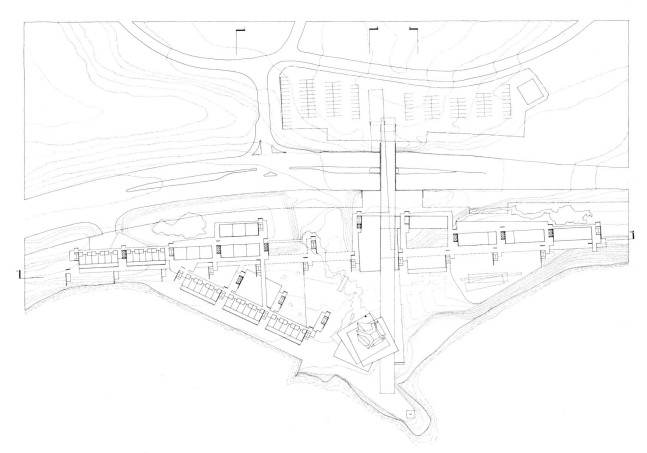

Floor plan of the employee
parking/service level.
Bottom, DD section.

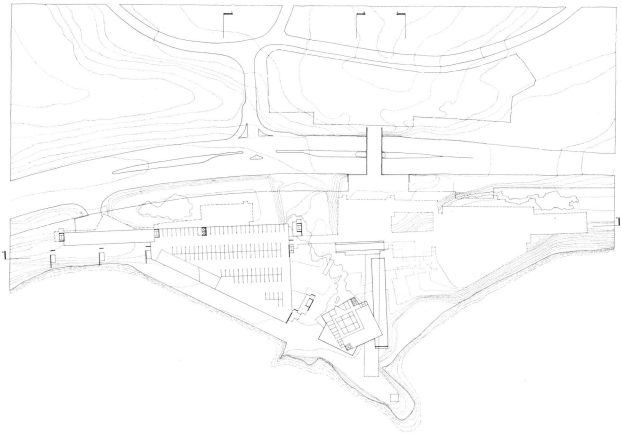

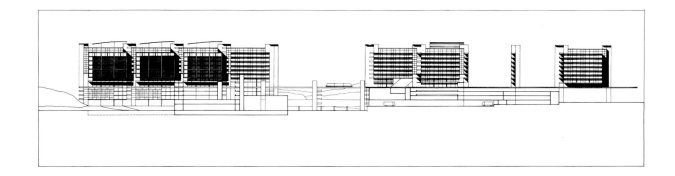

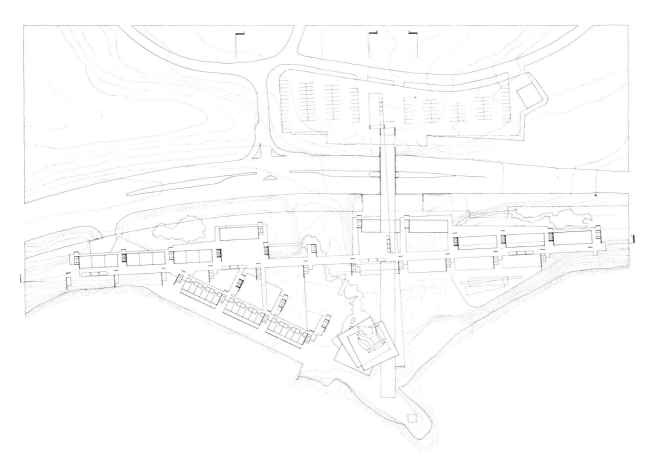

Floor plan of the main entry level and monorail level.

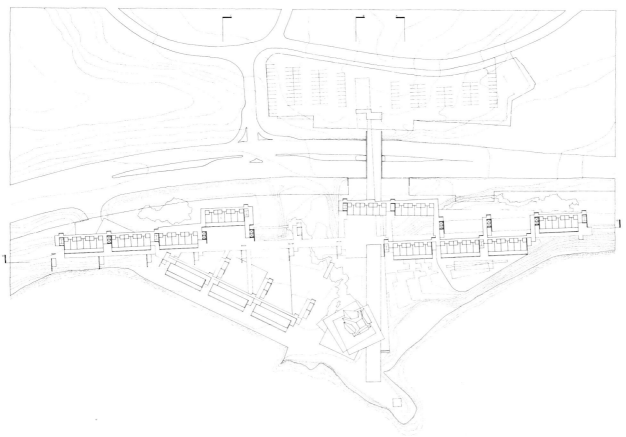

Floor plan of typical guest rooms level. Bottom, west elevation.

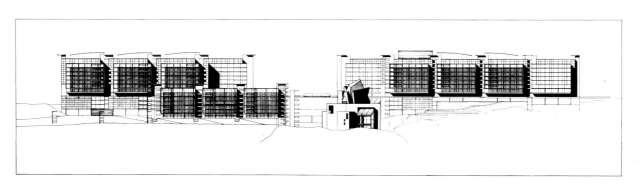

Exploded axonometric
view and, below, detail of
the model with the cultural
center Hookopu viewed
from loop road. Opposite
page, aerial view of the
model.

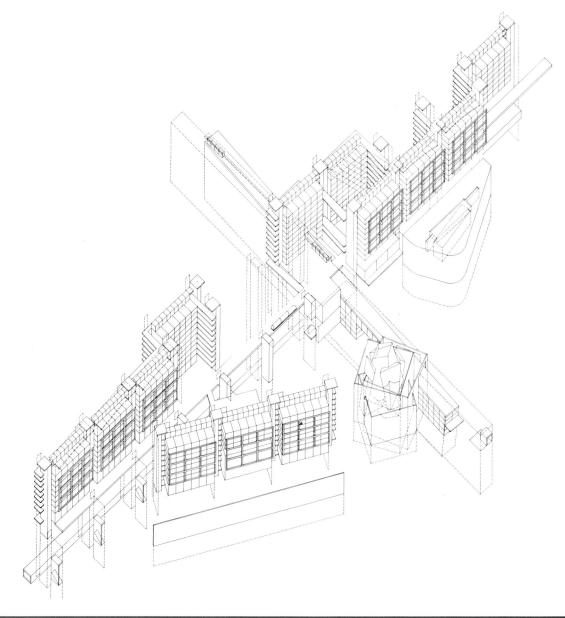

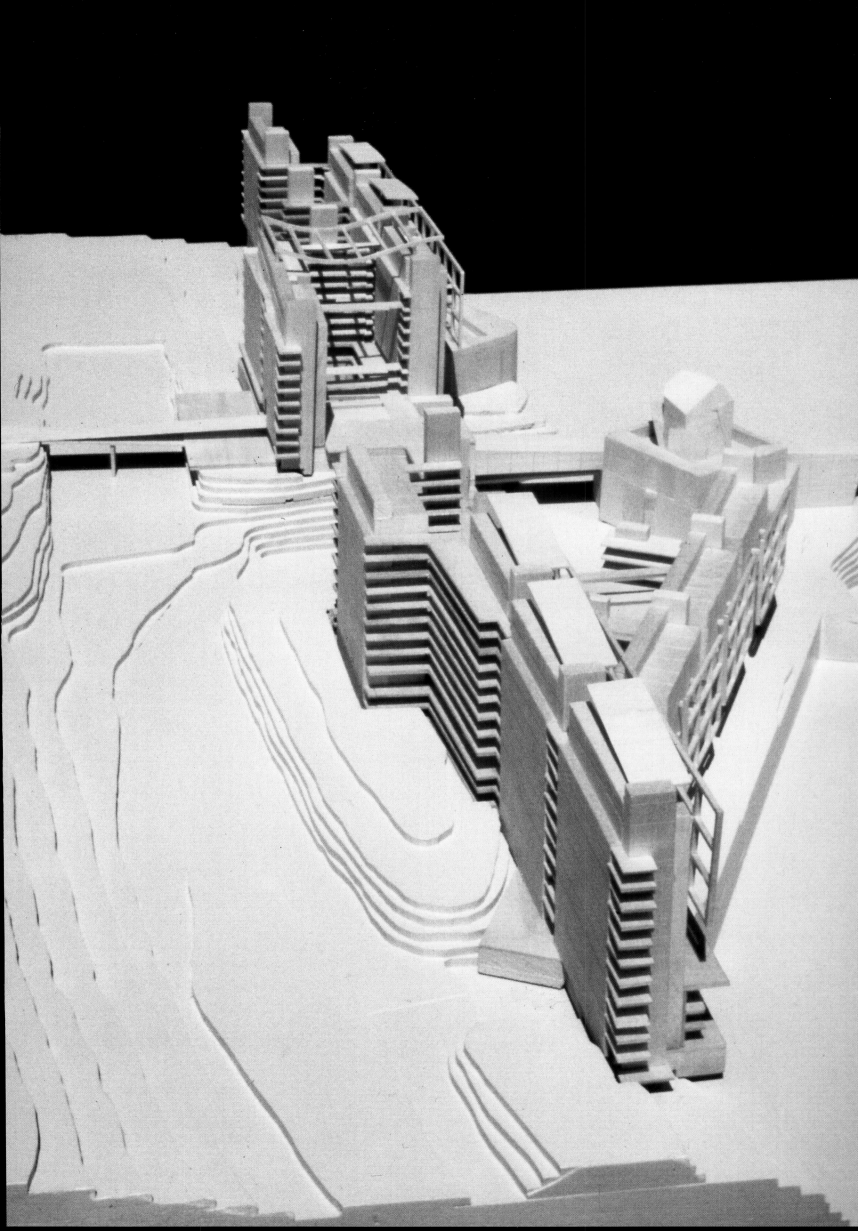

Live/Work Loft

A design/build collaboration between
Jon Frishman, Gregory Epstein, and Resolution: 4 Architecture

Location: New York City
Date of Completion: 1990
Square Footage: 1200 sq. ft.
Construction Cost: $20,000
Principals: Joseph Tanney,
Robert Luntz,
Gary Shoemaker

"And so the desire or need to bring in a third dimension gives rise to very simple artistic contrasts... Then the main action takes place in the middle, through its relation to the frontal planes 'behind and in front'".
Paul Klee

This is a home/office for an architect. This 1200 sq. ft. space is located in a renovated 1930's industrial loft building in the West Village of Manhattan and accommodates an architectural office of six as well as the residence of one of the partners. The project was initiated to explore a variety of concepts in the realm of the home/office within a very constricted budget.

This exploration of a new concept of the "railway flat" began by conceiving the public circulation as a series of sequential three-dimensional relocations that play against the existing structural columns. The 14' wide space becomes a reading of this relocation that defines the three Independent zones namely eating, sleeping, and working. This sequence is defined by full height enclosed volumes whose widths correspond to the module of a queen size bed/drafting board. As one progresses through the space, the Imprint of these volumes display three different column conditions. In the first condition, the volume encloses the column and allows only a partial reading of the column capital. In the second condition, the volume has shifted to reveal the column and only partially engages the capital while also defining an elevated bed platform. Finally, an exposed column demarcates the office proper.

The use of color serves to code various functional elements. Yellow shutters, which act as an aperture, define the amount of natural light that is admitted into the space, while red doors and movable flaps control privacy and ventilation. The volumes containing the elements of the living quarters are rendered in various shades of blue, green, and gray.

Exploded axonometric
view.

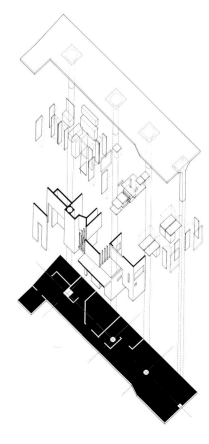

View from main entry.

View from office.

Perspective view of the
sleeping component.

Downtown Suffern
Multi-Use Redevelopment

Location:
Suffern, New York
Date of Design: 1991
Principals: Joseph Tanney,
Robert Luntz, Gary
Shoemaker
Structural Engineers:
Severud Associates:
Ed Massina, Ed Depaola
Consulting Engineers:
Jaros Baum & Bolles:
Mitch Simpler
Developer:
Talbert Berkman

Located 50 miles northwest of New York City, this project is sited along a railway right of way on a parcel in the center of the retail core of the village of Suffern. The program for this multi-use center consists of 40,000 sq. ft. of retail/commercial space, a 300 car parking deck and 48 units of affordable rental housing.

The downtown fabric of the village of Suffern is an interrupted one. It is a combination of a continuous two and three story street wall, built in the 1920's/1930's, with retail shops on the ground floor and residential and commercial on the upper floors. Coupled with this is a larger area of less defined blocks that are the result of the more recent developmental pressures of accommodating the car. The physical attributes of this earlier urbanity are quite memorable and are a point of departure for this project.

The project site, bounded by Chestnut Street and the railroad, is essentially the back/service side of the block on Lafayette Street. The design responds to the urban situation by clearly defining these two edges and thus establishes a sense of place. The L-shaped massing of the housing and retail components, in conjunction with the existing buildings on the site, creates a landscaped courtyard that is integrated with the parking structure. This architectural strategy also takes advantage of the outstanding views of the surrounding landscape and of the village of Suffern to the north and south. The traditional double-loaded corridor scheme has been shifted one bay along the corridor axis to create a variety of single and double-loaded entry conditions for the units. The layering of the facade allows for the incorporation of private terraces as well as sun control for the apartments. This shift, which is articulated by the modulation of the plan, section, and elevation of the housing units, recalls the energy and vitality of the passing trains.

Perspective view of the housing component and of the landscape courtyard at parking entrance.

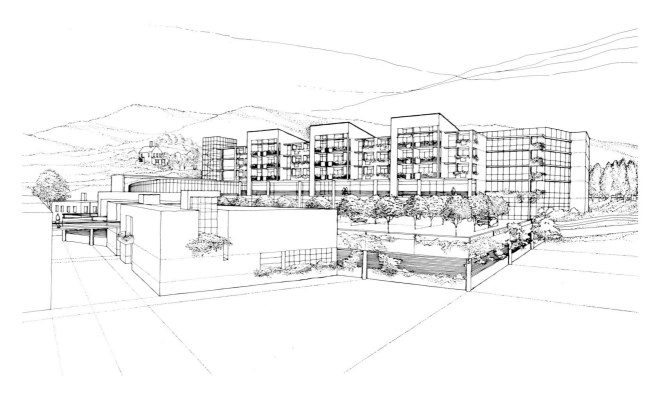

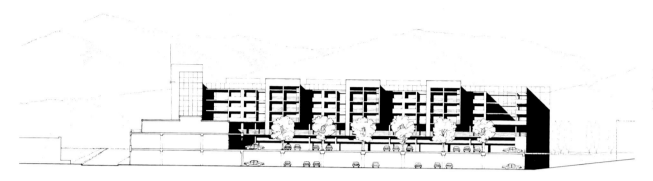

Longitudinal section/south
elevation, shadowed site
plan and cross section.

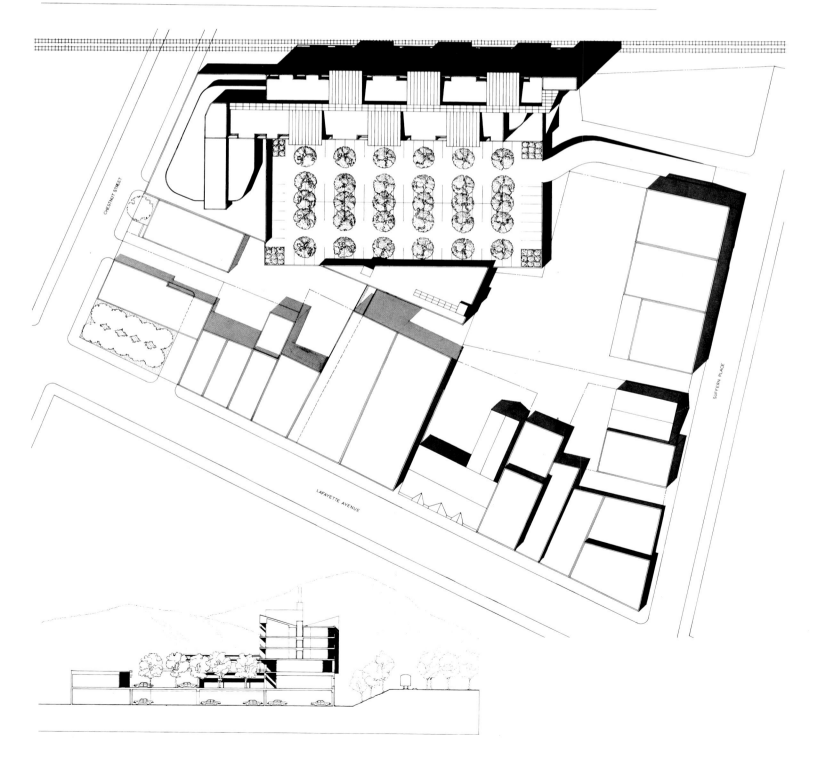

Below right, plan of level 1,
and left, plan of level 2,
above left, plan of level 3,
and right, plan of levels 4,5,
and 6.

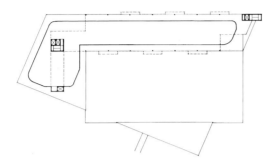
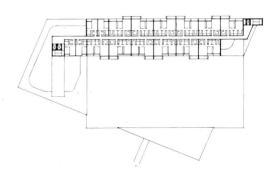

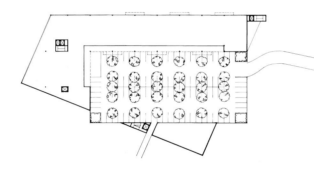
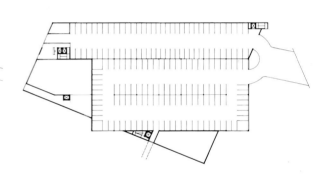

Perspective view of the
housing component with
the vehicle entry.

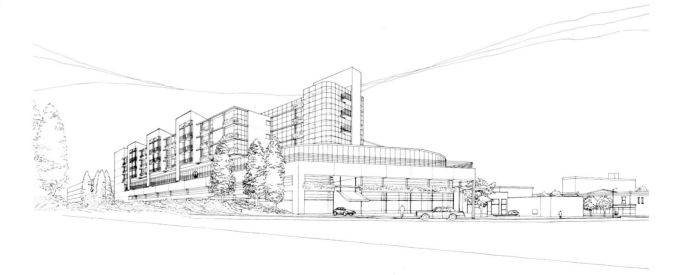

Aerial view of the model.

Ishino Schechter Loft

Location: New York City
Date of Design: 1991
Square Footage: 2000 sq. ft.
Principals: Joseph Tanney, Robert Luntz, Gary Shoemaker
Assistant: Casey S. Sherman

Located on 23rd Street in New York City, this 5th floor loft renovation is for a graphic artist of Japanese descent and her husband who is an independent TV producer. His recent work has focused on the events in South Africa, while she works for public television. The couple has one child.

After years of working in the entertainment and news media industries, they have amassed a sizable collection of memorabilia, which includes thousands of LP's, cassettes, CD's and books. Their collection also includes a number of South African and Japanese masks.

Conceptually, the design of the loft represents a landscape that reconciles aspects of two different value systems, namely Japanese minimalism and the vibrancy of South African colors and patterns.

The loft, which is a long, narrow, column-free space, has a north/south orientation. Since it is one floor higher than the roof of the adjoining buildings, the space receives northern, southern, and western light. To take advantage of this luminous attribute, and to address the client's shear quantity of "stuff", a design strategy of "packing" the perimeter is employed. This new intervention is a continuous storage element that visually connects all of the public spaces, entry, living and dining. This element is comprised of industrial components, namely bolted together steel channels and medium density fiberboard. Integrated with this system is a series of sliding colored plywood panels that modulate the shelving and on which the masks can be displayed. The entrance area is defined by a plywood meditation/storage platform. The center panel of the platform contains a cushion which allows the user to sit turning his/her back to the noise of the street below. The insertion of a new dressing element at the end of the dining space, constructed of metal studs, medium density fiberboard and glass, along with the incorporation of translucent sliding panels, enhances the sense of layering from entrance to the private domain. Finally, the incorporation of a mobile hearth, the overhead TV track, acts as another spatial connector, providing each space with a potential focus.

Site plan.

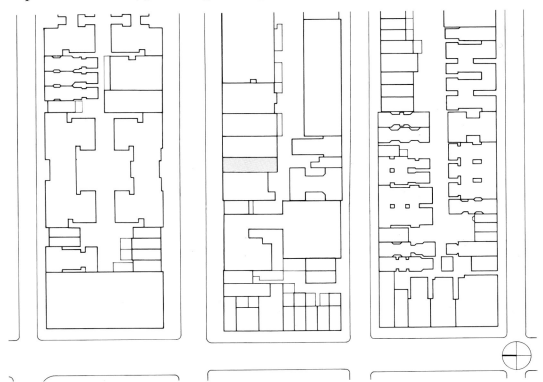

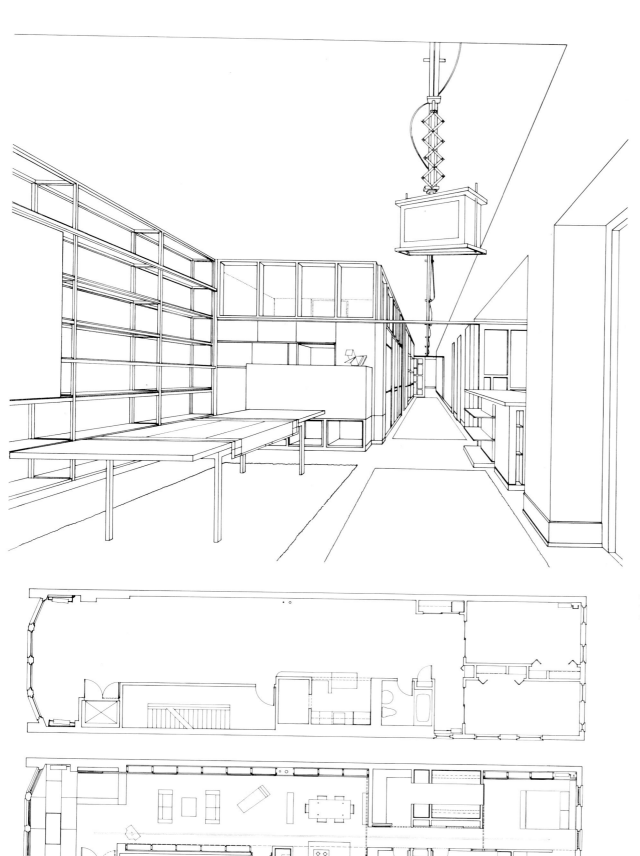

Interior perspective view
from dining room, showing
mobile hearth (TV).

Plan before and, below,
after intervention.

Interior perspective,
showing dressing/study
elements.
Bottom, details of the
model with the sliding
translucent panel of the
study and, at center, kit of
parts assembly.

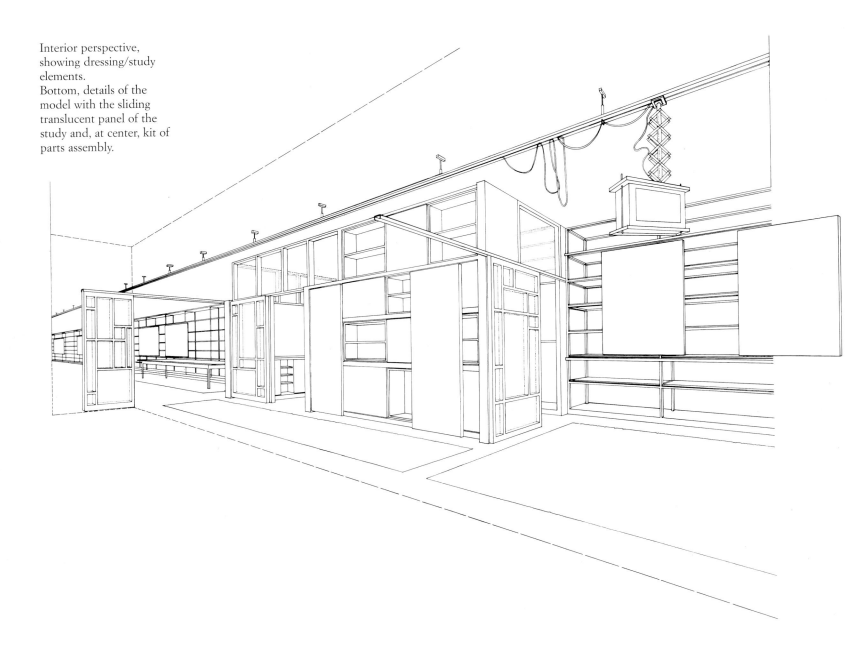

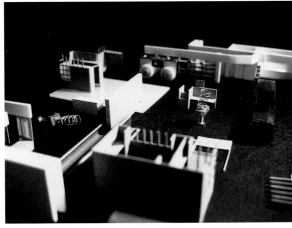

Exploded perspective view.

World Park

Location: Perth, Australia
Date of Competition: 1992,
Perth City Foreshore
Urban Design International
Competition
Principals: Joseph Tanney,
Robert Luntz, Gary
Shoemaker
Collaborator: Jim Doerfler
Consultant:
Dennis Ashbough

"Picturing others and everything which brings you closer to them is futile from the instant that communication can make their presence immediate".
Jean Baudrillard, "The Ecstasy of Communication"

During the night of February 20, 1962, John Glenn, orbiting the earth in the spaceship Friendship 7, described the lights of Perth to be clear and visible; thus, Perth became the first city to be recognized from space and connected to a worldwide network of instantaneous communication.

The concept of World Park is to bring Perth to the world and the world to Perth. The design process overlays traces of telecommunication waves along the landfilled area bounded by the city and the Swan River. The registration of the resulting images is the organizational device that defines the landscape elements of this public park. The orbital path of Friendship 7 is delineated by a line of lights arrayed in an axial relationship from Mt. Eliza to Harrison Island. The city grid was conceptually extended across the river, thus connecting the land and the water. Architectural elements are placed at the intersection of this extension and Friendship 7's orbital path. Coupled with the native Australian belief that the land is paper thin or merely floating on the water, this process allowed for the manipulation of the landscape through the removal or voiding of specific zones. Consequently, the water is exposed, and the nature of the landfill is revealed.

To further reinforce the concept of World Park, a number of real time monitors are situated throughout the park. These monitors would be linked to live broadcast images of other cities around the world in real time. These objects of technology become focal points analogous to the fountain/statue of more traditional public spaces. World Park and Perth become a major node in a global communication network connected via electromagnetic waves.

Wave diagram shown with site registration.

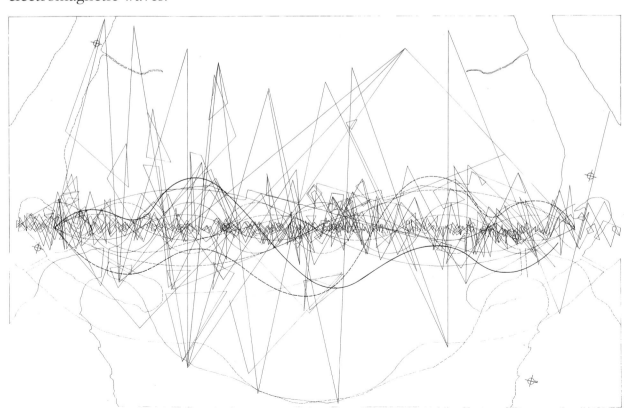

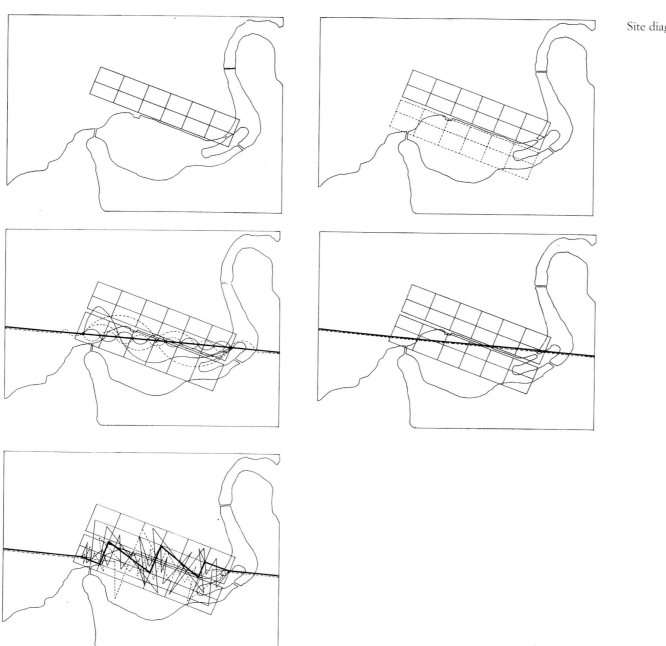

Site diagrams.

Left, the boat house; right,
the aquarium. Below,
overall view showing
existing narrow bridge in
context with the new
intervention.

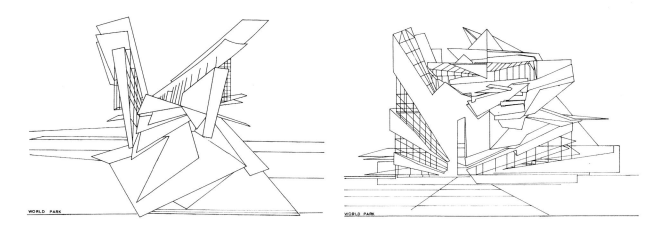

WORLD PARK   WORLD PARK

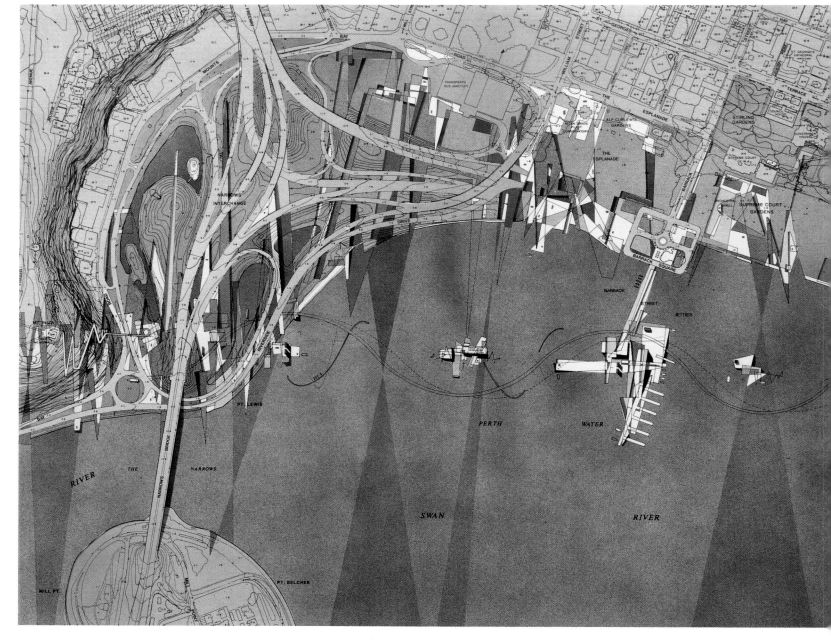

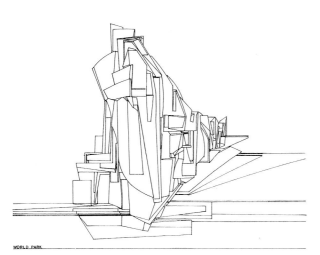
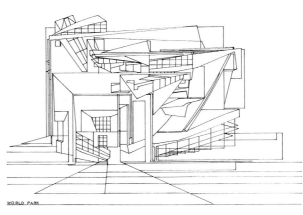

Left, technology museum; right, information/perform pavilion.

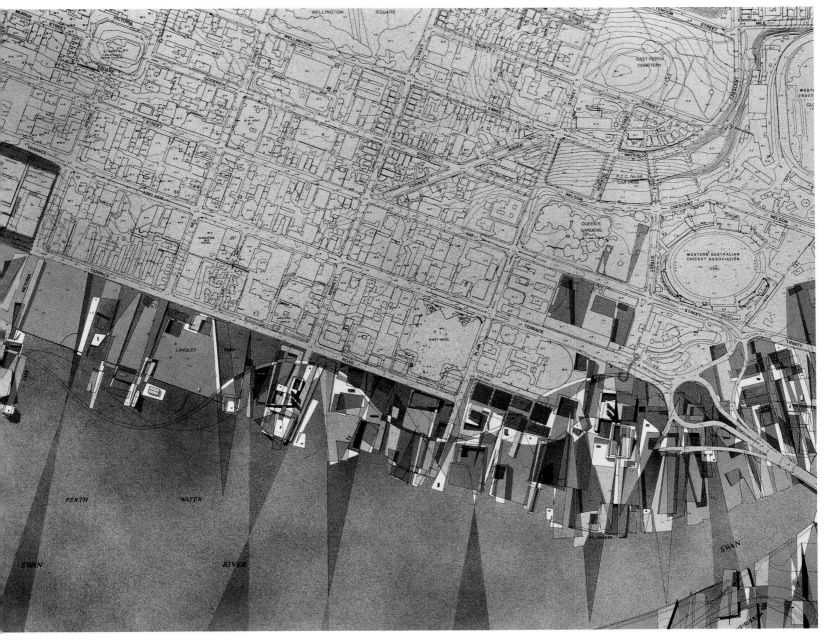

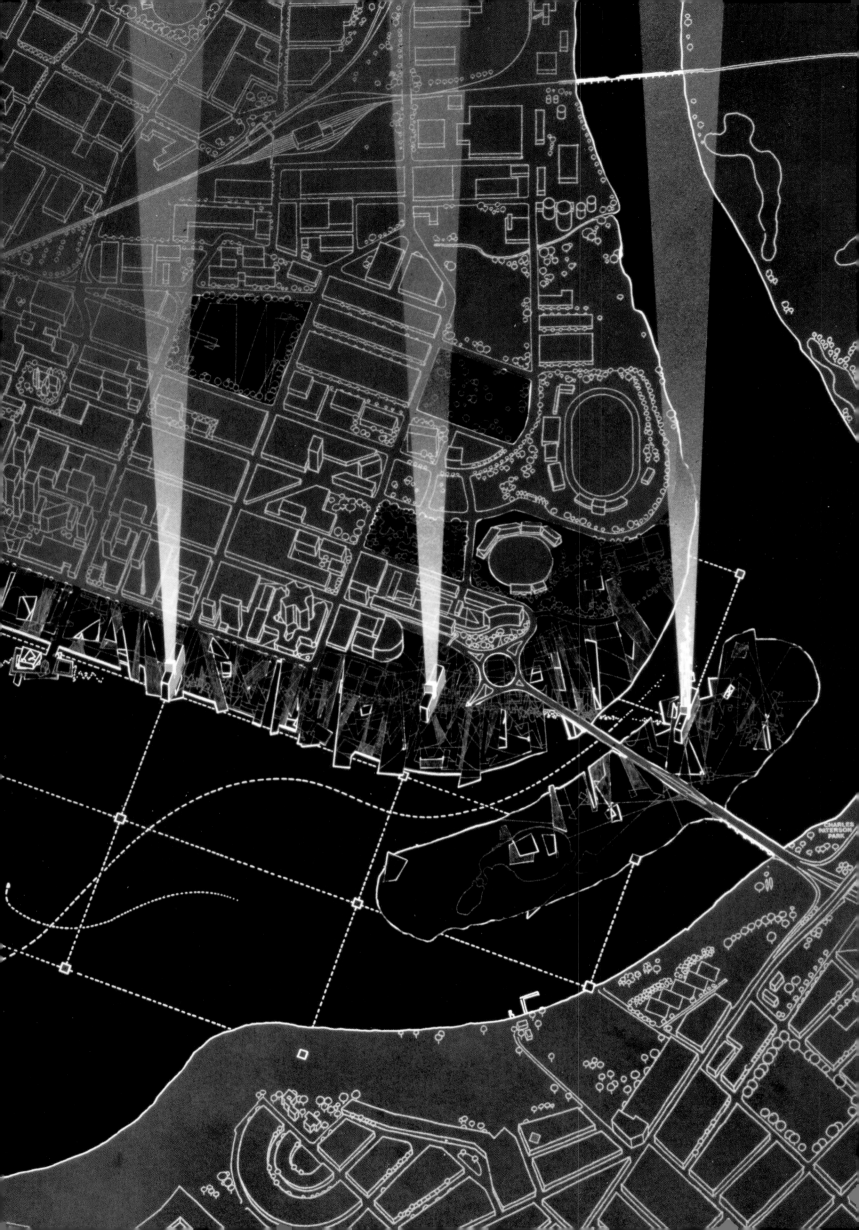

CHARLES
PATERSON
PARK

Convention Hall

Location: Nara, Japan
Date of Competition: 1992,
Nara Convention Hall
International Design
Principals: Joseph Tanney,
Robert Luntz, Gary
Shoemaker
Competition Collaborators:
Tom Lewis, Mel Felix

"But the paneled room folded itself through a dozen impossible angles, tumbling away into cyberspace like an origami crane".
William Gibson, "Neuromancer"

The design of the Nara Convention Hall attempts to become a symbiosis of Nara's history and future. The historical essence of Nara, as exemplified in the Noh drama, the tea ceremony, and floral arrangement, embodies the notion of presentation. Upon its completion, the Hall will be the centerpiece of the Nara urban redevelopment program. The future role of the Convention Hall as an international cultural center is analogous to the urban redevelopment's role as a gateway to Nara. This relationship is re-presented as a two dimensional site text that articulates a proposed future. In the traditional Japanese artform of origami, a three dimensional volume/space is produced through the cutting and folding of a two dimensional text. Embodying this idea of presentation, the site text is manipulated through a series of reflections and folds, to create a three dimensional symbol for Nara.

This method of architectural production has allowed for a non-traditional manifestation of the theater morphology. The origami exploration allows the program elements and interstitial spaces to be woven into a bar typology. This resultant form is skewered by a glass enclosed circulation system that forms an edge of the urban plaza and allows entry to the convention hall.

Perspective view of initial massing study.

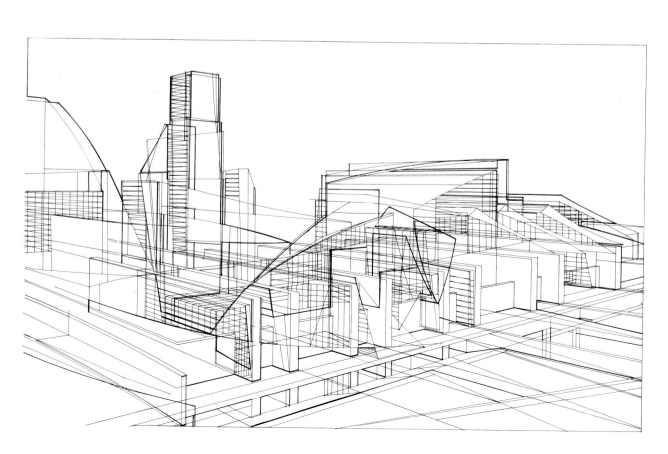

Site plan.

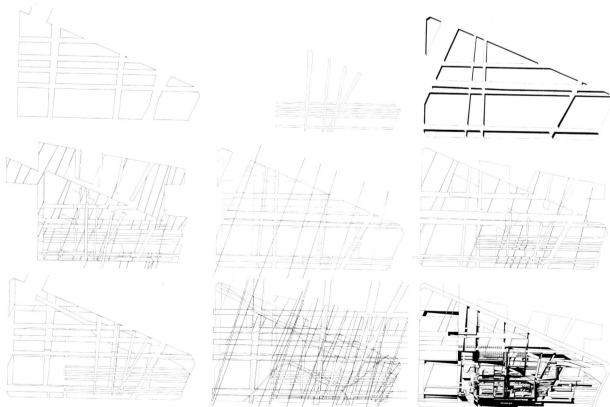

Site diagrams.

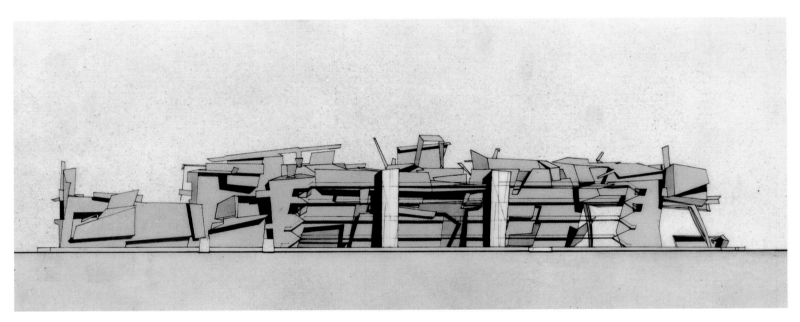

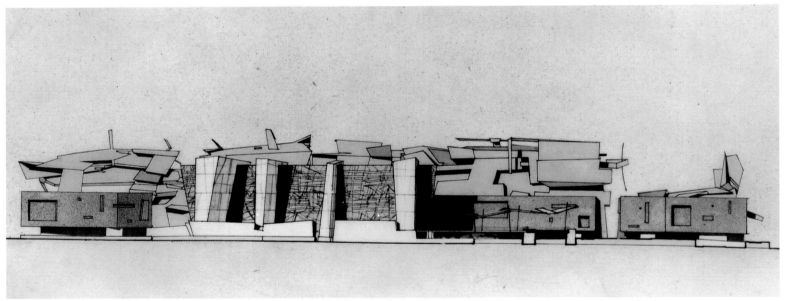

Top of page, elevation from
service street and, below,
elevation from urban park.

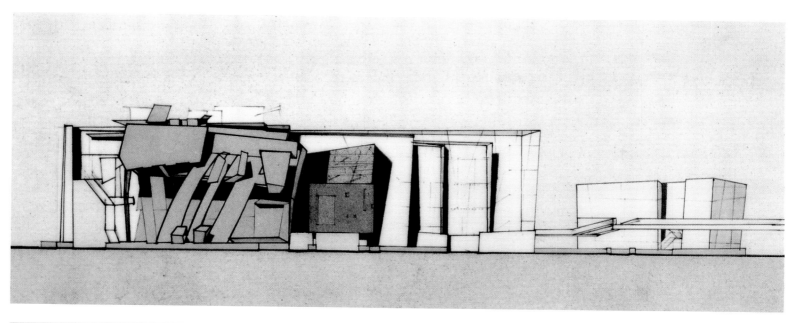

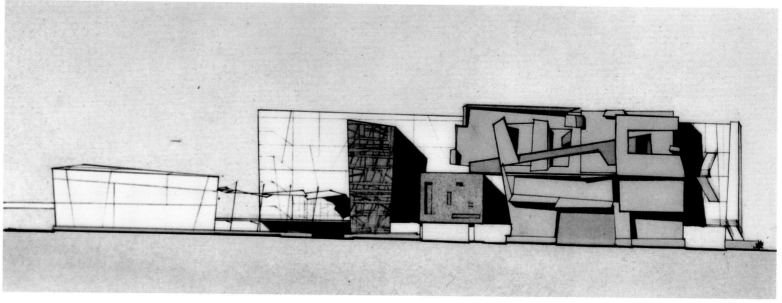

Top of page, elevation from
small hall and, below,
elevation from amphitheater.

Floor plans.
Opposite page, aerial
perspective view showing
urban park at lower left.

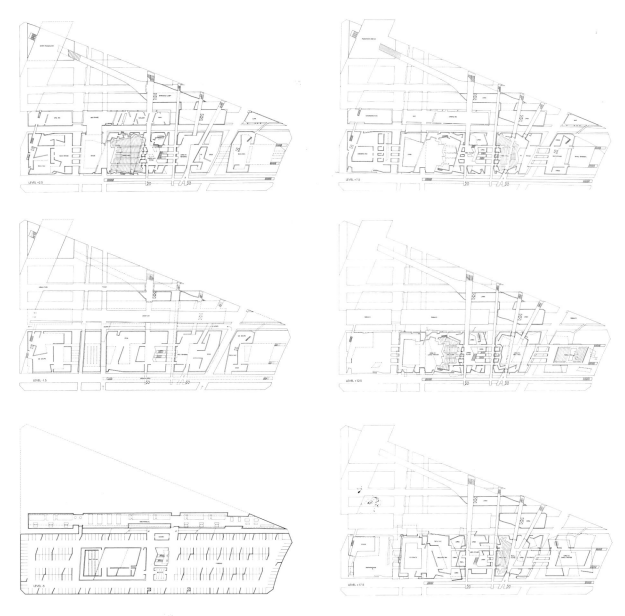

Longitudinal section
through large/medium/
small halls.

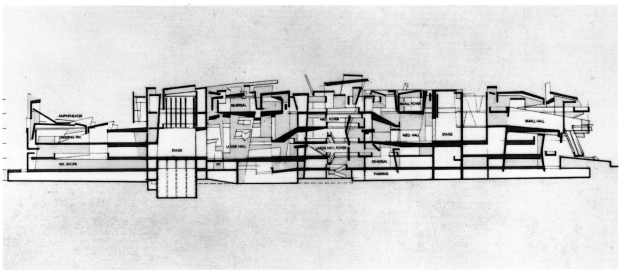

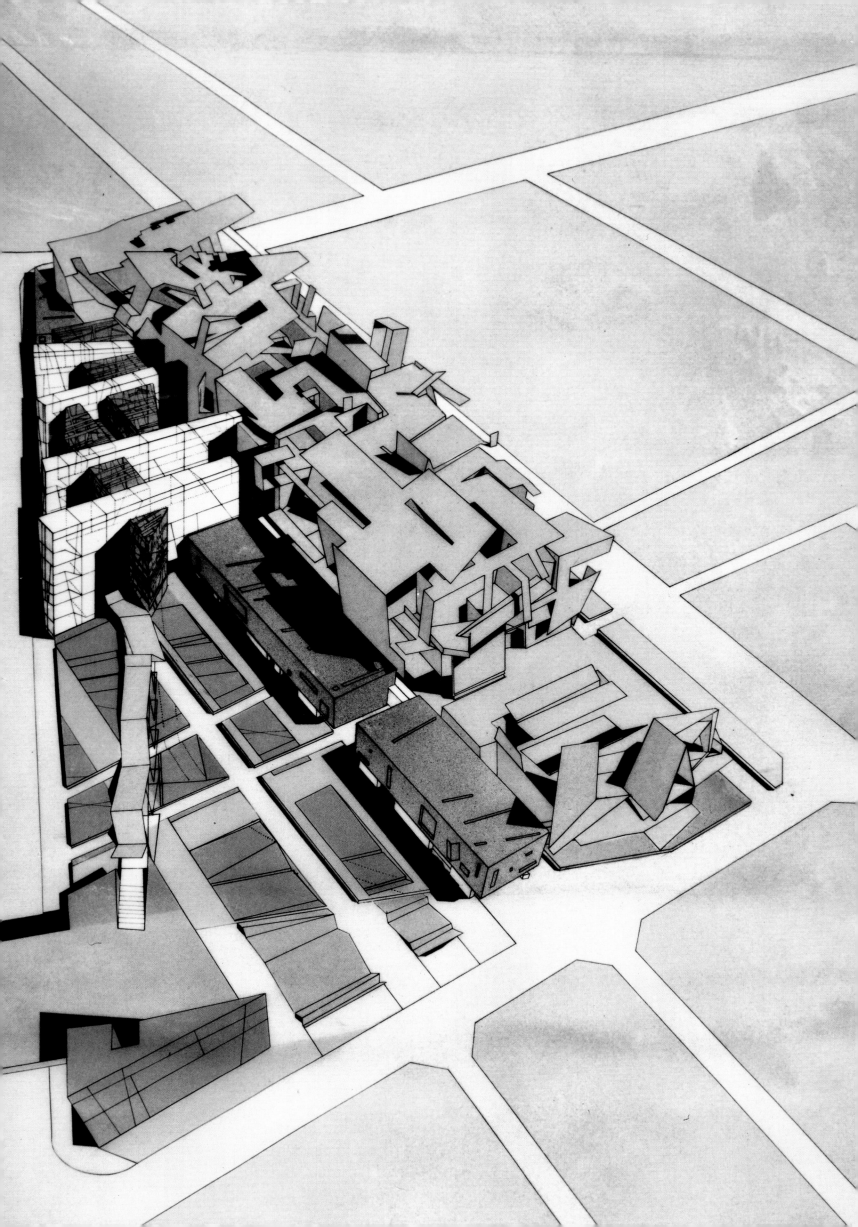

Simint Fashion Corp.

A collaboration between Resolution:4 Architecture
and Glenn Rescalvo Design Studio

Location: New York City
Date of Completion: 1993
Square Footage: 2700 sq. ft.
Principals: Joseph Tanney,
Robert Luntz,
Gary Shoemaker
Consulting Engineers:
Hannington Engineers
Contractor:
John Gallin & Sons

Simint Fashion Corp., a new subsidiary of Simint SpA, the Modena based sportswear company, had outgrown the 5th Avenue showroom/office space it was sharing with the parent company. In relocating to a 3000 sq. ft. space within the same building, Simint Fashion Corp.'s architectural program included four main components: private offices, a buyers showroom, a collection storage space, and a bullpen space for account management.

The new showroom, located in a horizontally compressed space typically found in newer office towers, has northern and eastern exposures. The design intent was twofold: to provide a strong corporate identity by organizing the program elements to structure the work environment, and to make a visual connection with the horizon. Simint's identity is tied to the process of creating, producing, and promoting Franco Moschino's especially whimsical line of casual sportswear. To represent this architecturally, an arcing wall that distinguishes the public and private zones of the showroom was introduced as the primary spatial organizing element. This wall also establishes an identifiable corporate graphic.

This blue seam, curved in plan and tilted 5 degrees in the z axis, describes a dis-splayed wall floating between the ceiling and floor planes. The sweeping curve acts as a circulation edge that draws people from the entry to the showroom. The wall modulates this procession, first by compressing the space against the glass edge of the offices, then releasing and visually extending the space of the showroom into the city beyond. The wall also provides for display of the current sportswear line. To emphasize the interplay of materials, an investigation that could show both a handcrafted and an industrial richness was undertaken. The sign of the hand is most evident in the bowed blue plastered wall.

The industrial components that comprise the tectonics of the private offices are "off-the-shelf" unprimed steel tubes that support floor-to-ceiling sand blasted sheets of glass. The steel tubes have a clear lacquer finish. This industrial aesthetic acts as a counterpoint to the plaster wall's handcrafted texture. The Arne Jacobsen chairs and the Noguchi tables in the showroom also reinforce the company's sensitivity toward the craft of built objects.

Site/location plan.

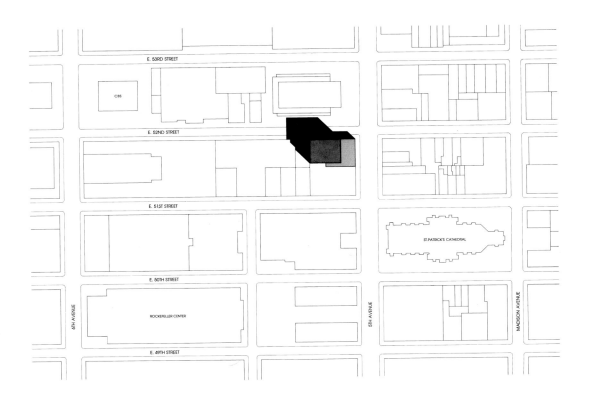

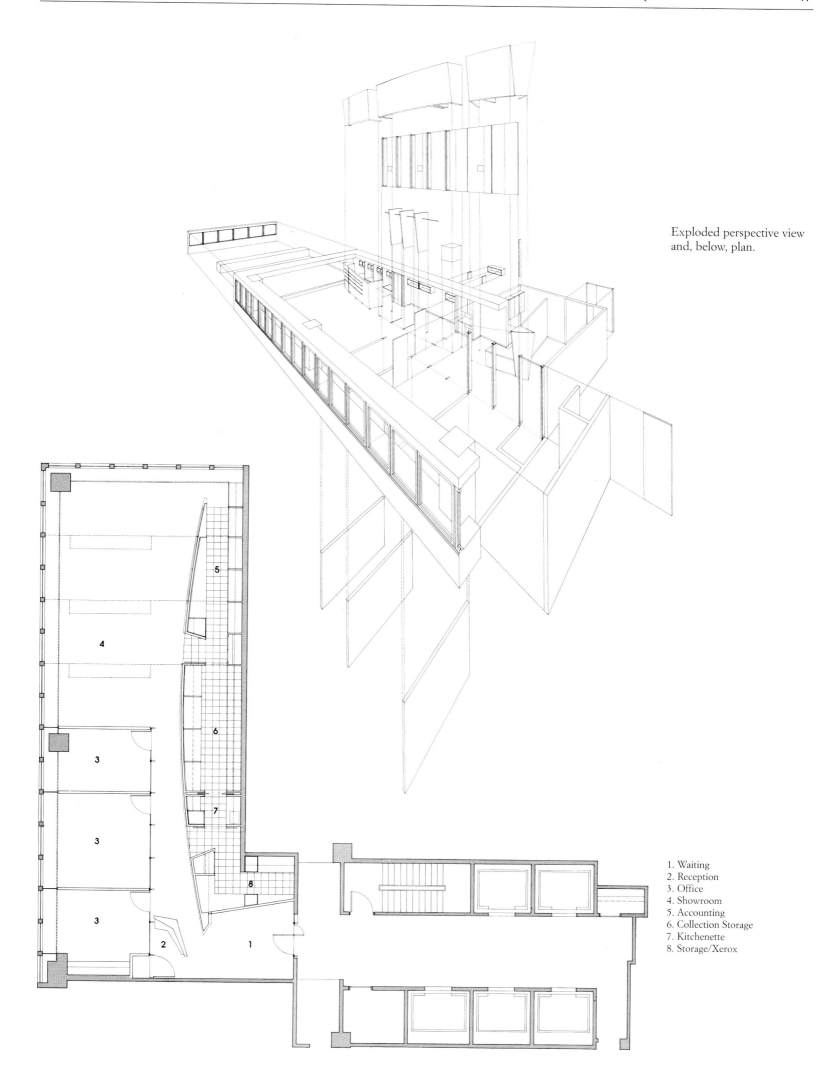

Exploded perspective view
and, below, plan.

1. Waiting
2. Reception
3. Office
4. Showroom
5. Accounting
6. Collection Storage
7. Kitchenette
8. Storage/Xerox

View from the showroom
of the integral colored
plaster curved wall.

View from the stainless steel "end cap" of the integral colored plaster wall.

View from the reception toward the showroom. Sandblasted sheets of glass provide privacy for the offices on the left.

View from the showroom.

McCann-Erickson Worldwide Art Studio

Location: New York City
Date of Completion: 1994
Square Footage: 4300 sq.ft.
Principals: Joseph Tanney,
Robert Luntz,
Gary Shoemaker
Project Team: John DaCruz,
Casey S. Sherman
Contractor: StructureTone

McCann-Erickson, an international advertising agency, commissioned Gwathmey Siegel to design its New York offices in 1987. Since then, we have been asked to "update" a number of smaller, isolated pockets within the 300,000 sq.ft. facility.

Originally designed to accommodate the mechanical artist, the art studio quickly became obsolete in its ability to accommodate the expanding role and needs of the computer artist. Obvious conflicts and contrasts between low tech/high tech, old/new, dirty/clean, bright/dark, and marker/mouse became issues requiring attention.

How does an aging, down & dirty, 24 hr-a-day art studio gradually transform itself into a computer lab of the future? Consistent only in that it is in a constant state of flux, this transformation is acknowledged in the organization and use of the studio. The main space is arranged in a horseshoe configuration, taking advantage of the existing three exposures by pushing private and semi-private workstations to the perimeter, allowing communal storage and work surfaces to occupy the center. The perimeter is layered with a continuous Isoduct system of power and communication capable of sustaining spontaneous access and future technological growth.

Each desk is a 6-0' x 2-8' "slab" of plastic laminate mounted on pedestal files equipped with casters, allowing the opportunity to "roam" and the flexibility of group arrangement. Modular storage units were designed with casters as well and parked under the stationary work surfaces. These containers hold flatfiles, supplies, and vertical art work.

Exploded perspective view
of typical computer
workstation.

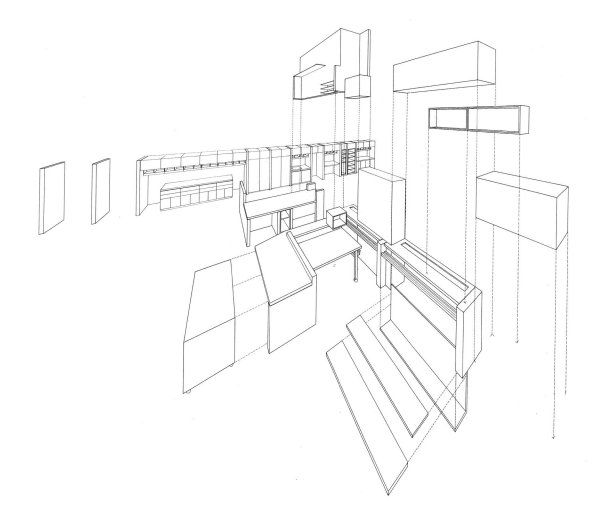

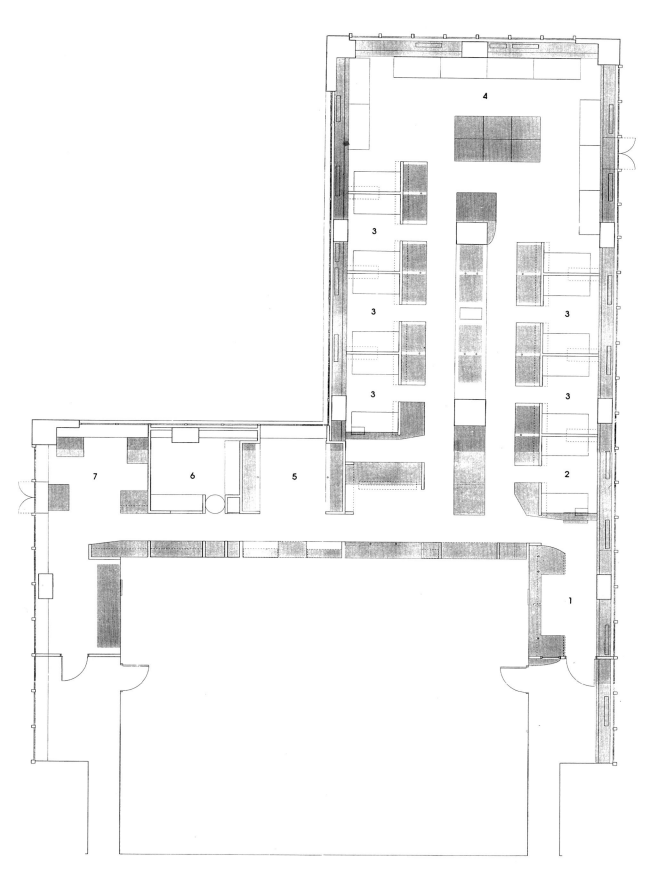

Floor plan.

1. Reception
2. Administrative Director
3. Computer Workstation
4. Swing Space
5. Conference
6. Dark Room
7. Mechanical Artists

Exploded perspective view
of computer workstation,
storage components, and
movable art storage bins.
Below, view showing
movable art storage bin
units.

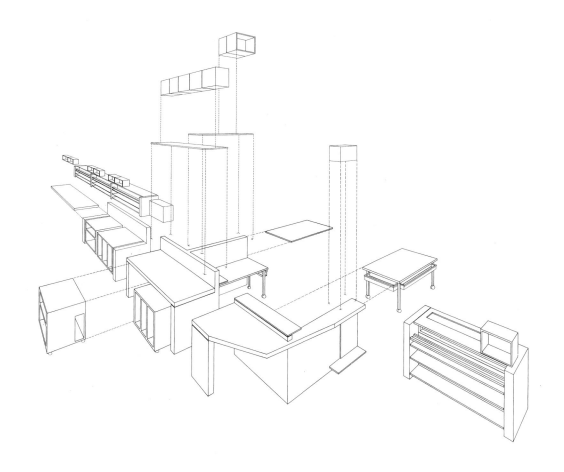

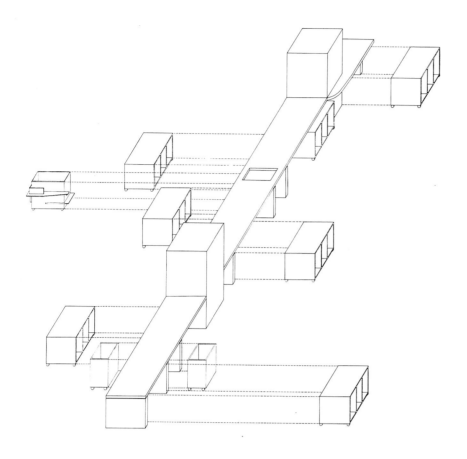

Isometric of movable art storage bins.
Below, view looking towards swing space.

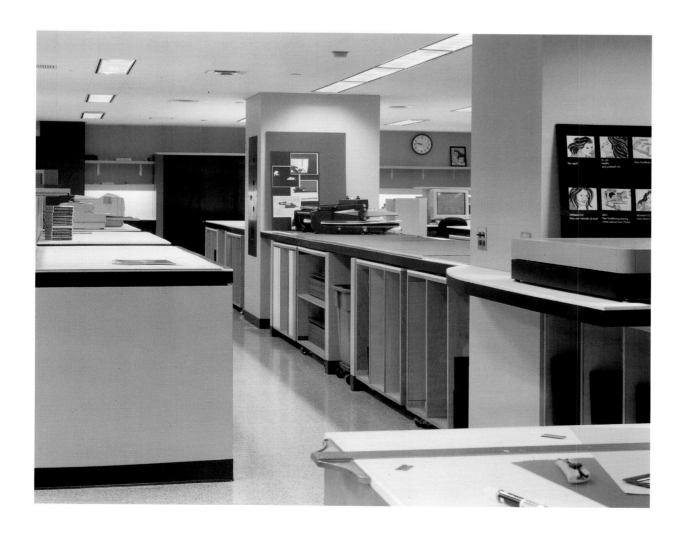

Head Start

Location:
Hightstown, New Jersey
Date of Completion: 1994,
Head Start Facility Design
Competition
Principals: Joseph Tanney,
Robert Luntz,
Gary Shoemaker
Project Team:
John DaCruz,
Casey S. Sherman

Located in central New Jersey on rural land outside a small town and in clear view of the Turnpike, the site for the new Head Start facility sits ironically down the road from a prep school. Linked by a stream, which is symbolically full and plentiful near the prep school, and shallow and struggling near the Head Start facility, the two sites are representative of their schools serving two very different segments of the population.

The design for the model Head Start facility attempts to metaphorically slip beyond these boundaries by establishing a pattern of overlapping segments with the intention of strengthening the link between different elements. From this direction, the pre-engineered building develops from the inside-out, revealing a simple concept capable of being reinterpreted for any site specific context. Beginning with addressing the needs of the children, the classroom is seen as a module which is repeated to form a bar or "zone of learning". Each classroom is layered perpendicularly with a skylight knitting it with a parallel bar or "zone of parenting/teaching", which includes nutrition, social, and health services. This link symbolizes not only the encouraged active participation of the parents, but also Head Start's comprehensive program. The skylight slips creating zones of circulation and zones of storage. This pattern of overlap establishes the major element of an L scheme completed by an object containing the multipurpose room.

These two elements become site specific by forming an entry court containing a ramp leading one into the building and providing a direct view through to the playground, stream, and woods beyond. The roof floats above the classrooms gently bowing upward acknowledging the scale of the Turnpike in the distance, while the multipurpose room is situated in direct correspondence with the apex of the stream and relates in scale to the neighboring town. The use of skylights, clerestories, and oversized windows provides views out of the facility, allowing the children a sense of connection to their surroundings. The abundance of natural light and views of the sky represent growth and new beginnings, even unlimited possibilities, access to the stars inspiring the child's spirit of "dare-to-dream" - perhaps even the opportunity to attend the prep school down the road.

Site plan.

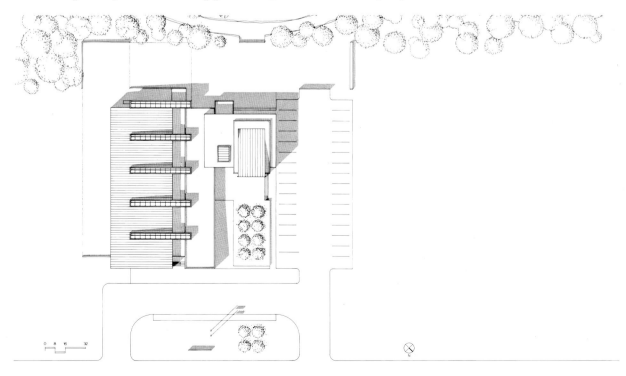

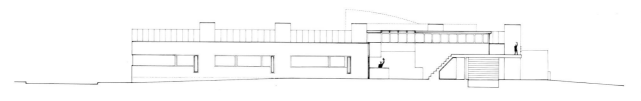

From top down: entry
court elevation/section
through play ground
overlook; classroom
elevation; section through
skylight/entry elevation;
section through
classroom/mainentry/
multi-purpose room.

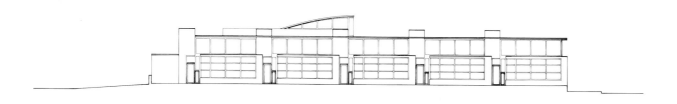

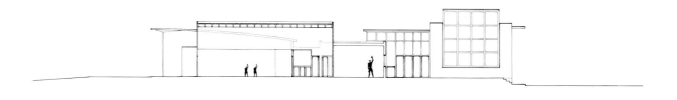

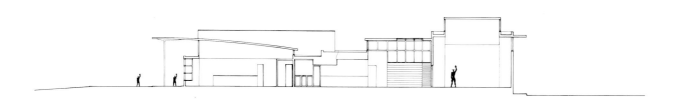

Floor plan.
Below, axonometric view of
a typical classroom module.

Education
1. Classroom
2. Children's storage
3. Cot storage
4. Teacher's storage
5. Wet area
6. Children's bathroom
Staff Support
7. Conference/Workroom
8. Laundry room
9. Maintanance room
Family Service/
Parent Involvement
10. Parent training
room/Computer room
11. Parent lounge
Social Services
12. Office
Multi-purpose Area
13. Multi-purpose area room
14. Stage
15. Storage
Administration
17. Site supervisors' office
Nutrition
18. Kitchen
19. Pantry/Storage
Health Services
20. Examining room/Screening
room
21. Sick bay/Office
Playground
22. Play area-Hard area
23. Play area-Soft surface
24. Storage
Transportation
25. Entry court
26. Main entry
27. Playground overlook
28. Children's drop off
29. Children's entry
30. Parking
31. Service drop off

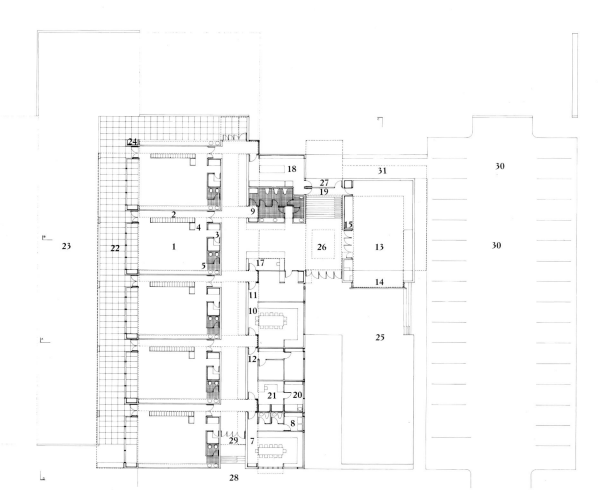

Model view showing classroom element.

Aerial view of model showing main entry.

Edgemere Community Center

Location:
Queens, New York
Date of Completion:
1960 original,
1994-1996 renovation
Square Footage:
14,000 sq.ft.
Principals: Joseph Tanney,
Robert Luntz,
Gary Shoemaker
Project Team: John DaCruz,
Casey S. Sherman,
Eric Liftin (Project
Architect)
Modelmakers:
Kevin Bergin,
Mario Gentile,
Jeffrey Dvi-Vardhana

This project is the result of an RFP submission to the New York City Housing Authority. The funding for the renovation is from the 1993 Federal Comp. Grant II Community Center Program.

The Edgemere Houses, constructed in 1960, consist of 24 six story residential buildings located on two adjacent blocks in Queens, New York. The one story community center comprises approximately 14,000 sq. ft., and is attached to two of the multi-story residential buildings. The main architectural features of the Community Center are the entry vestibule and the gymnasium. These two elements are distinguished by their taller massing and by the incorporation of architectural terra cotta as an exterior cladding material.

A goal of this modernization is to instill a sense of pride within the Edgemere community as well as restoring the architectural integrity of the original structure. Due to the diversity of the center's programs and its function as a community magnet, the existing entry is redesigned to create an inviting image. The new stainless steel and glass block canopy provides protection from the elements as well as allowing sunlight to illuminate the entry during the day. The canopy also incorporates a series of uplights/downlights to dramatically illuminate the entry at night as well as affording a sense of security. The use of direct burial lights along the entry paths also illuminate the existing terra cotta panels of the gymnasium. The landscape design reinforces the natural pedestrian circulation of the site as well as creating a defined edge for the existing structure.

To allow for the simultaneous usage of the center by both the seniors and the day-care children, some of the interior spaces have been reorganized to provide the appropriate separation. A defined separate entry and ramp is incorporated for the seniors. To meet the projected food service needs of the center, the existing kitchen has been upgraded to commercial standards. The existing panty is to be upgraded to meet the needs of the senior and day-care children populations. All of the existing building systems will be upgraded or replaced and many of the interior finishes will be replaced to help strengthen the center's visual image. This modernization program attempts to restore the status of the community center as a vital entity within the Edgemere neighborhood. To see the look on the kids' faces, when told of the possibility of the center's renovation, reminded us that as architects, we can make a difference.

Floor plan showing paving pattern.

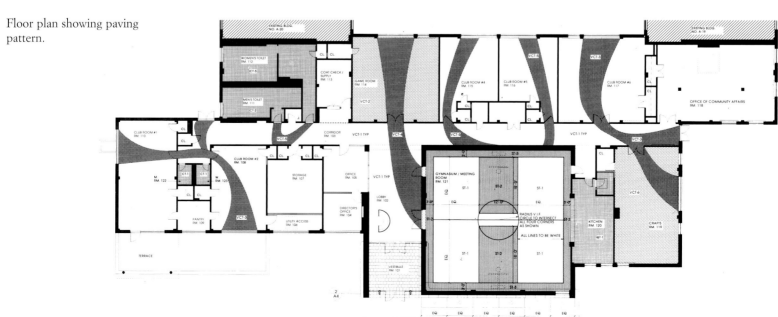

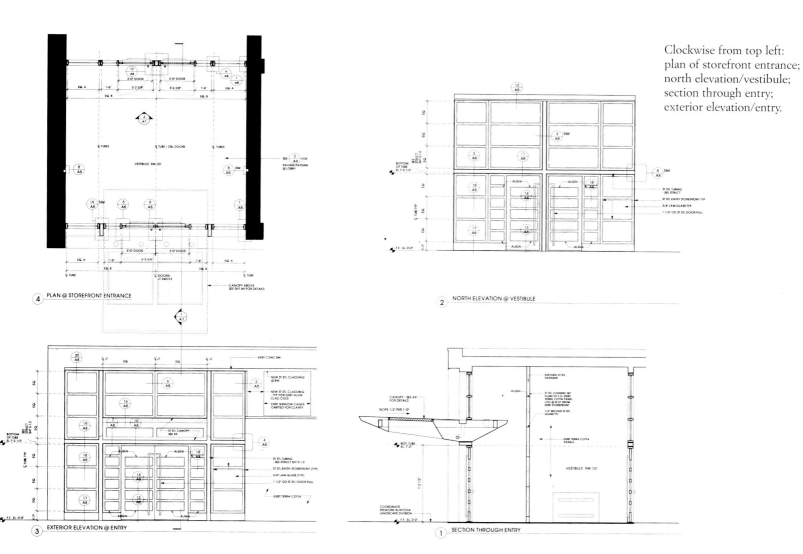

Clockwise from top left: plan of storefront entrance; north elevation/vestibule; section through entry; exterior elevation/entry.

4 PLAN @ STOREFRONT ENTRANCE

2 NORTH ELEVATION @ VESTIBULE

3 EXTERIOR ELEVATION @ ENTRY

1 SECTION THROUGH ENTRY

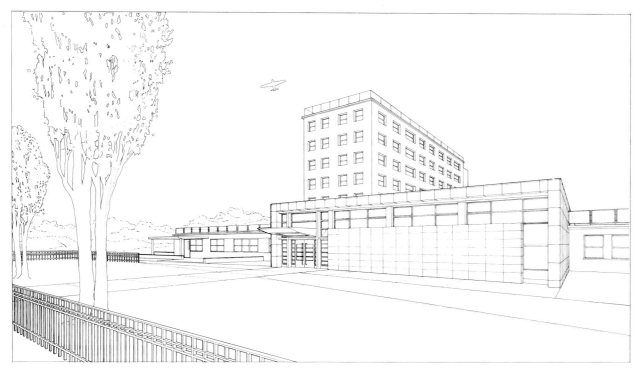

Perspective view showing main entry with new canopy/storefront.

Model: view of gymnasium
showing concrete waffle
slab roof structure and,
below, view of main entry
canopy/storefront.

Model: partial view of gymnasium with concrete waffle slab at ceiling and, below, view showing interior storefront/ reception desk at entry.

Premier Health Club

Location:
Hallandale, Florida
Date of Completion:
October 1995
Square Footage: 16,000 sq.ft.
Principals: Joseph Tanney,
Robert Luntz,
Gary Shoemaker
Project Team:
John DaCruz, David
Schilling, Markus Bader,
Eric Liftin
Collaborator:
Paul Boardman
Modelmakers:
Kevin Bergin,
Mario Gentile,
Jeffrey Dvi-Vardhana,
Erin Vali
Contractor:
Ray Luhta Construction

This total-health club concerns itself with all aspects of fitness, incorporating freeweight training, cardiovascular and Cybex machines, massage, testing, aerobics classes, and nutrition. The facility occupies a two-story space at the base of an 11-story office building.

The club comprises multiple functions, some public and some private, which work together to support the fitness of its members. Our scheme divides the space into zones to separate office building from club and private from public. These divisions, realized as colored, monolithic walls, are modulated by compositions of punched openings, which make visual and circulatory connections between zones. Visual play thus links programmatic areas and experiences to tie together disparate activities into a unified conception of fitness.

Spatial games are complicated by the introduction of program requirements as objects into the major spaces. Sponsoring such functions as a pro shop, a juice bar, and a membership office, these kiosks are carved superimpositions of commerce within a larger field of athletic activity.

The project's visual language uses a vocabulary of planes which wrap and carve space. The rhythms of these planes, which can veil, reveal, or reflect, bind the different areas into a single composition and frame the athletes in a dynamic setting. The incompletion of carved or exploded forms fosters ambiguity between adjacent spaces and allows the rhythm of planes to continue through all the spaces.

Surface materials reflect our interest in bringing inexpensive, off-the-shelf materials into a refined environment. One major wall is lacquered fiberboard while the others are textured gypsum board. A raked, low plywood ceiling defines a main corridor. Light is bright but softened by inverting the hung industrial fixtures to face the ceiling. The stair is a typical steel fabrication, but an illuminated landing and surrounding soffits and openings create a dramatic ascent.

Second level plan.

1. Circulation/entry
2. Workout
3. Test/Fitness
4. Office
5. Massage
6. Mechanical
7. Aerobics

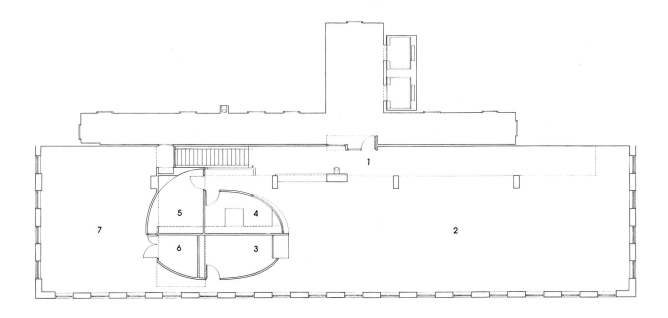

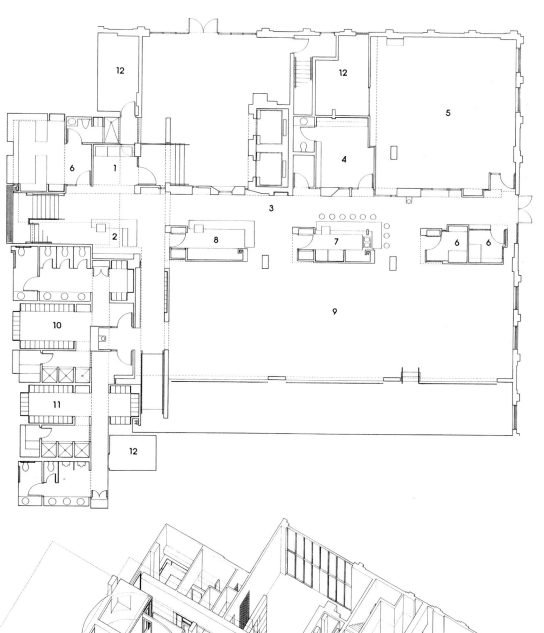

Lower level plan.

1. Main entry
2. Reception
3. Circulation
4. Day Care
5. Aerobics
6. Office
7. Juice Bar
8. Pro Shop
9. Workout
10. Women's locker
11. Men's locker
12. Mechanical

Axonometric view.

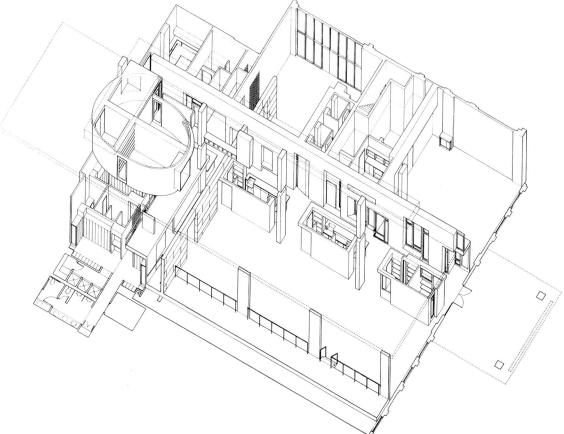

Exploded perspective of office area.
Opposite page: view of reception/main stair and, below, detail of the entry at aerobics room.
Next pages view of circulation zone from reception showing the three program elements (pro-shop, juice bar, offices) in perspective.

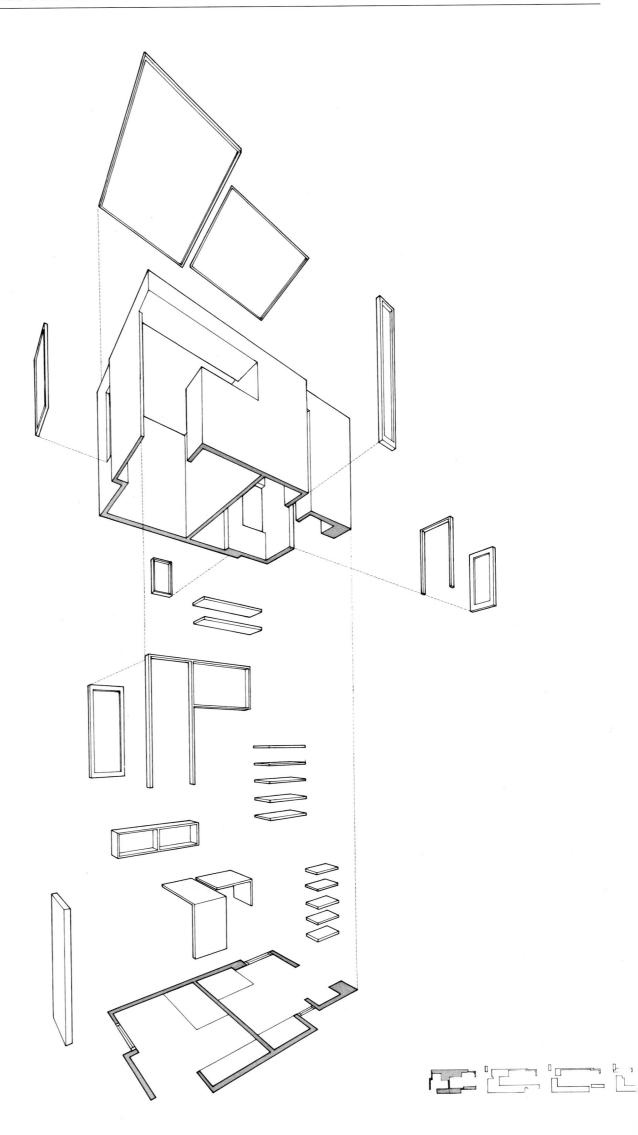

Finkelstein Residence

Location:
Cornwall-On-Hudson, NY
Date of Completion:
1997 (estimated)
Square Footage: 8500 sq.ft.
(including renovation of
existing house)
Principals: Joseph Tanney,
Robert Luntz,
Gary Shoemaker
Project Team: John DaCruz
(project architect), Heather
Roberge, Clay Collier,
Eric Liftin, Setu Shah,
Jennifer Pereira,
Mario Gentile,
Jeffrey Dvi-Vardhana,
Kevin Bergin

We read a site in terms of geometry, topography, ecology, and visual paths. Architectural form can arise by analogy or metonymy, where the elements of a site are repeated, transformed, or reinterpreted in a different medium. Architecture can also respond more reciprocally to site conditions, without drawing formal relationships between the site and intervention.

The rural setting of Cornwall-on-Hudson inspires an architecture which engages the site without mimesis. In fact there is a double site, the existing vernacular buildings and building foundations as well as the larger environment of sloping land and mature trees. The house design employs a correspondence between the new construction and the existing built elements white reciprocating the gestures of the landscape.

The existing compound comprises several simple structures in an informal relationship. The new intervention forms a figure Z, which makes connections to the existing components while framing new courtyards and new relationships. The front of the Z is composed to forge formal relationships with the site, to articulate the compound's more public face. The rear is more informal, to support a relaxed country life.

The foundation of an old, bulky garage becomes a garden terrace, a middle ground of staged natural growth. A new, smaller garage spins off to create a new relationship between the main house, an existing barn, and the entry drive. The new main house is placed on the intersection of the terrace/garage and the existing main house. Voids between the new house and the flanking structures become entrances, which allow an experience of the relationship between old and new, as well as breaking up the building mass and giving views through the landscape.

The most prominent gesture of the new house is a parabolically curved "lobe". This protruding, glazed room gives panoramic views of sloping lawn, trees, and a pond. It extends to include kitchen and hearth, to incorporate most functions of family life. Upstairs, bedrooms are arranged to accomodate privacy while allowing for the care of young children. Built-in storage helps to modulate the spaces while a rhythm of variously curved roofs provide spatial drama and light. Outdoor terraces provide elevated positions to experience the landscape. The second floor spaces open to various sides, to focus on specific areas of the landscape, such as Storm King Mountain, which was previously not visible from the house. Thus, movement through the house stimulates a continual discovery of built space and of the dramatic landscape beyond.

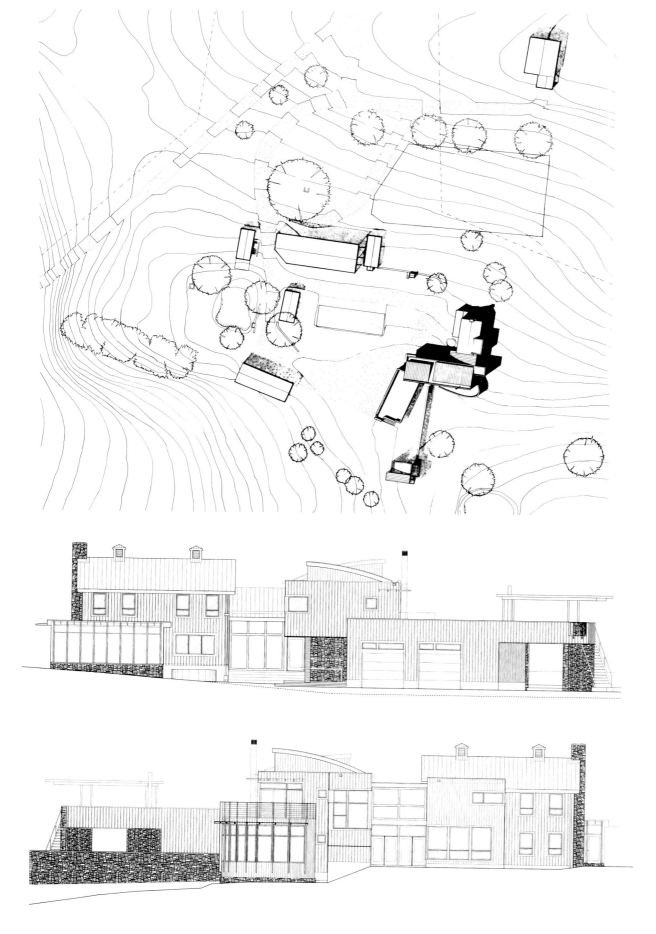

Site plan showing barns and new house and, below from bottom up: south rear elevation and north entry elevation.

Aerial view of the model from the west.

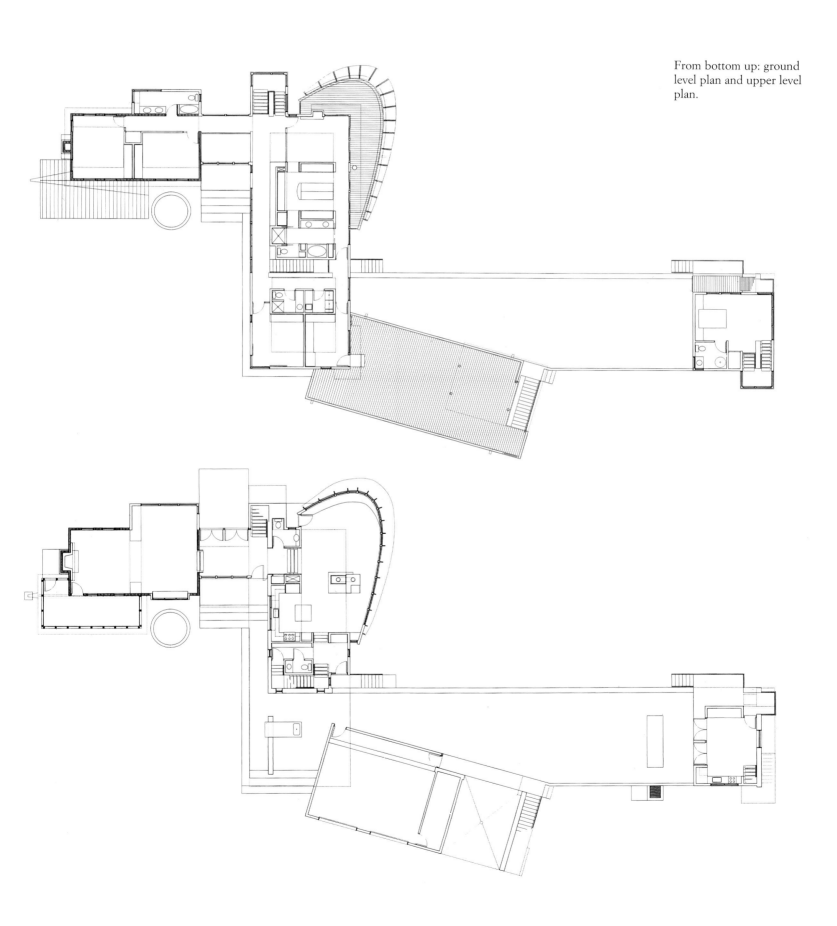

From bottom up: ground level plan and upper level plan.

Section through main entry
and, below, section through
family room/master
bedroom.

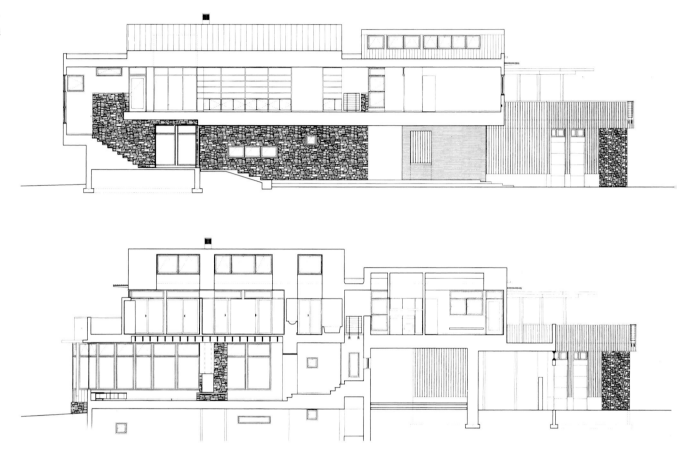

Details of working
drawings.

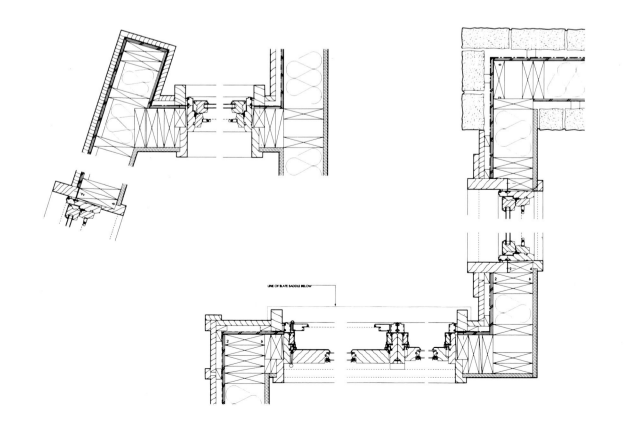

LINE OF SLATE SADDLE BELOW

Model showing the guest house in foreground and glassed family room at background.
Below, aerial view of the model from south-west.

Stackless Library

Location: Evanston, IL
Date of Completion:
1991, Evanston Public
Library Competition
Principals: Joseph Tanney,
Robert Luntz,
Gary Shoemaker
Collaborator:
David Fratianne
Structural Engineers:
Severud Associates:
Edward Messina,
Edward Depaola
Consulting Engineers:
Jaros Baum & Bolles:
Mitch Simpler

"Electric technology is reshaping and restructuring patterns of social interdependence and every aspect of our personal life. It is forcing us to reconsider and re-evaluate practically every Thought, every action, and every Institution taken for granted. Everything is changing". Marshall McLuhan

This project was for the Evanston public library competition. Evanston is a suburb of Chicago, and the site is in a residential area located a few blocks from Lake Michigan. The site contains the existing library that was to be removed according to the program brief. The program also called for the traditional library requirements such as stacks, research areas, exhibition space, and typical support and technical spaces. It was in this project that we challenged the idea of what a library could be in this information age. We saw this as an architectural opportunity to express society's evolving relationship with today's ever changing technology.

In 1853, Victor Hugo wrote that the printed book killed architecture. No longer was architecture required to record the historic events of civilization. The printing press now allowed for a more efficient and economic means for the mass production of Information. Based on 18th and 19th century precedents, a library could be seen in terms of housing cultural information. Unlike a museum which is typically a haven for original works of art valued for their uniqueness, a library contains copies of cultural information that are widely distributed. This suggests a static sheltering of information, that is oriented to paper technology.

Because of the effects of technology, new demands will be placed on the library typology. Today, the electronic media allows for almost instantaneous access to information. It allows for individual interaction with information. The notion that a library function as a secured repository of books was viewed obsolete. Therefore, without the requirement to store books, the library became stackless. It becomes an interactive center for electronic information access/retrieval, a cultural billboard promoting technological browsing and research. The new library engages the existing library. The obsolete structure was not to be removed, but enshrined as a museum of a bygone era of information retrieval.

This project questions the library's traditional building typology and formal resolution since it is no longer a repository of books, but a machine for information. Conceptually the new space in which this information exists no longer requires large bays to shelter it. The steel/concrete slab structural bay of 30'x36' allows for a single loaded corridor scheme accommodating VDT/computer terminals and circulation. The exterior curtain wall, comprised of vision glass panels and sandblasted glass, light weight composite graphite panels, translucent panels, and video monitors, was viewed as an information wall that can display in real time, the research and browsing taking place on the interior, as well as local and worldwide events.

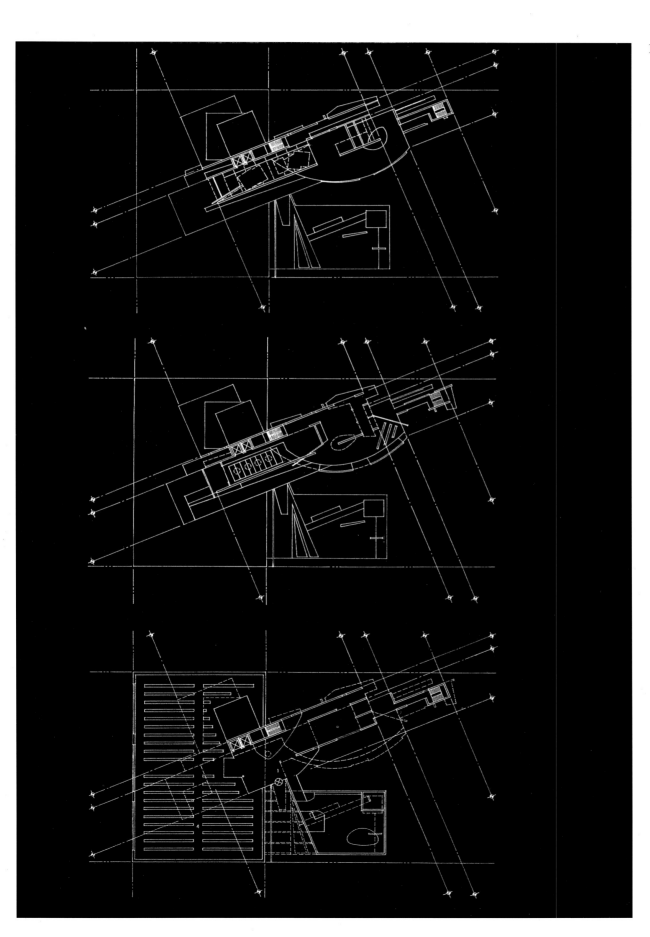

Floor plans.

Site plan.

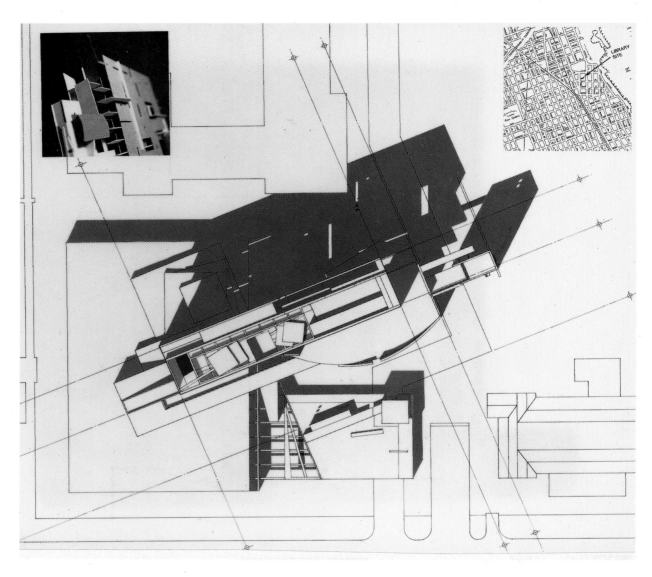

Perspective view showing
existing library and the new
intervention. Model view
showing existing context.

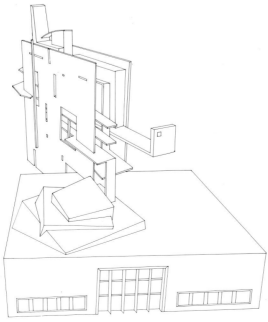

Model view: detail of rear drop-off entry.

Project List 1990-1996

1990

Wainaku Mill Hotel	Hilo, Hawaii
WNET Planning Study	New York, NY
Neurogenetics Laboratory	Paramus, NJ
WNET Graphics Suite	New York, NY
Ishino/ Schechter Loft	New York, NY
Resolution:4 Offices	New York, NY
Molloy/Ertinghausen Residence	Mt. Pocono, PA

1991

Buckingham Residence	Salem, OR
Petrich Residence	Seattle, WA
McClean Apartment	Brooklyn, NY
Stackless Library	Evanston, IL
Suffern Multi-Use Development	Suffern, NY
717 5th Avenue Lobby Design Study	New York, NY
Braque Cafe Design Study	New York, NY

1992

Bridgeport Masterplan	Bridgeport, CT
Jones Residence	New York, NY
McCann-Erickson 6th Fl. Personnal	New York, NY
McCann-Erickson 15th Fl. Conf.	New York, NY
McCann-Erickson Bowen's Office	New York, NY
McCann-Erickson Dooner's Office	New York, NY
McCann-Erickson 22nd Fl.	New York, NY
Perez Residence	Caguas, Puerto Rico
Clark Residence	New York, NY
McCook Bowling Center	Dayton, OH
Convention Hall	Nara, Japan
World Park	Perth, Australia

1993

McCann-Erickson 19th Fl. Art Studio	New York, NY
Osborn Residence	Pelham, NY
Simint Fashion Corp.	New York, NY
Miller Residence	New York, NY
Cohen Residence	New York, NY
Goodman Residence	Damariscotta, ME
Hilton Residence	New York, NY
Jenike/Tabibian Residence	Stuart, FL
Sopher Residence	New York, NY
Spreebogen Competition	Berlin, Germany
Dream House with No Style	Suburbia, USA
Accion International	Miami, FL
Vogle Residence	Miami, FL

1994

Thomas Residence	Miami, FL
Behrmann Residence	Miami, FL
Edgemere Commercial Center	Far Rockaway, NY

Malin Kitchen — New York, NY
St. Paul's Book & Media Center — Miami, FL
Head Start Preschool — Hightstown, N J
Babushkin Dental Office — Trumbell, CT
Stuart Residence — New York, NY
Flumenbaum Residence — New York, NY

1995
McCann-Erickson 3rd Fl. — New York, NY
McCann-Erickson Upgrade — New York, NY
Mourin Residence — Miami, FL
Miami Baptist Association Clinic — Miami, FL
Daily Food Food Bank — Miami, FL
O'Brien Residence — Brooklyn Heights, NY
Premier Health Club — Hallandale, FL
Arden Residence — New York, NY
Hanika Residence — Miami, FL
Finkelstein Residence — Cornwall on Hudson, NY
Tiden Residence — New York, NY
Educational Video Center — New York, NY
Vincent Residence — New York, NY
De Giorgis Residence — New York, NY
Premier Chiropractic — New York, NY
Finkelstein Loft — New York, NY
IRRI Laboratory — Miami, FL

1996
Malin Residence — New York, NY
Zaofong Universe Lobby — New York, NY
St. Martin's Press — New York, NY
Franco Residence — Brooklyn Heights, NY
Amster Yard Art Studio — New York, NY
McCann-Erickson 16th Fl. Upgrade — New York, NY
McCann-Erickson Bathrooms — New York, NY
60 Pineapple Street — Brooklyn Heights, NY
Allston Residence — Brooklyn Heights, NY
Cohen Residence — Brooklyn Heights, NY
Vickers Residence — Manhasset, NY
5th Ave Salon — New York, NY
Brandt Residence — New York, NY
Jack Vickers Residence — Manhasset, NY
Danly Residence — Miami, FL
Neree Residence Master Plan — Miami, FL
St. Elizabeth Church Master Plan — Keller, TX
1250 East Bldg. Cafeteria Relocation — Miami, FL
Lawyers Office — Miami, FL
1250 East Bldg. Lobby Renovation — Miami, FL
Jacoby Residence — Miami, FL
Vexlund Residence Master Plan — Miami, FL
Spyro Residence — Long Island, NY
McCann Travel Agency — New York, NY